URNEMOUTH.

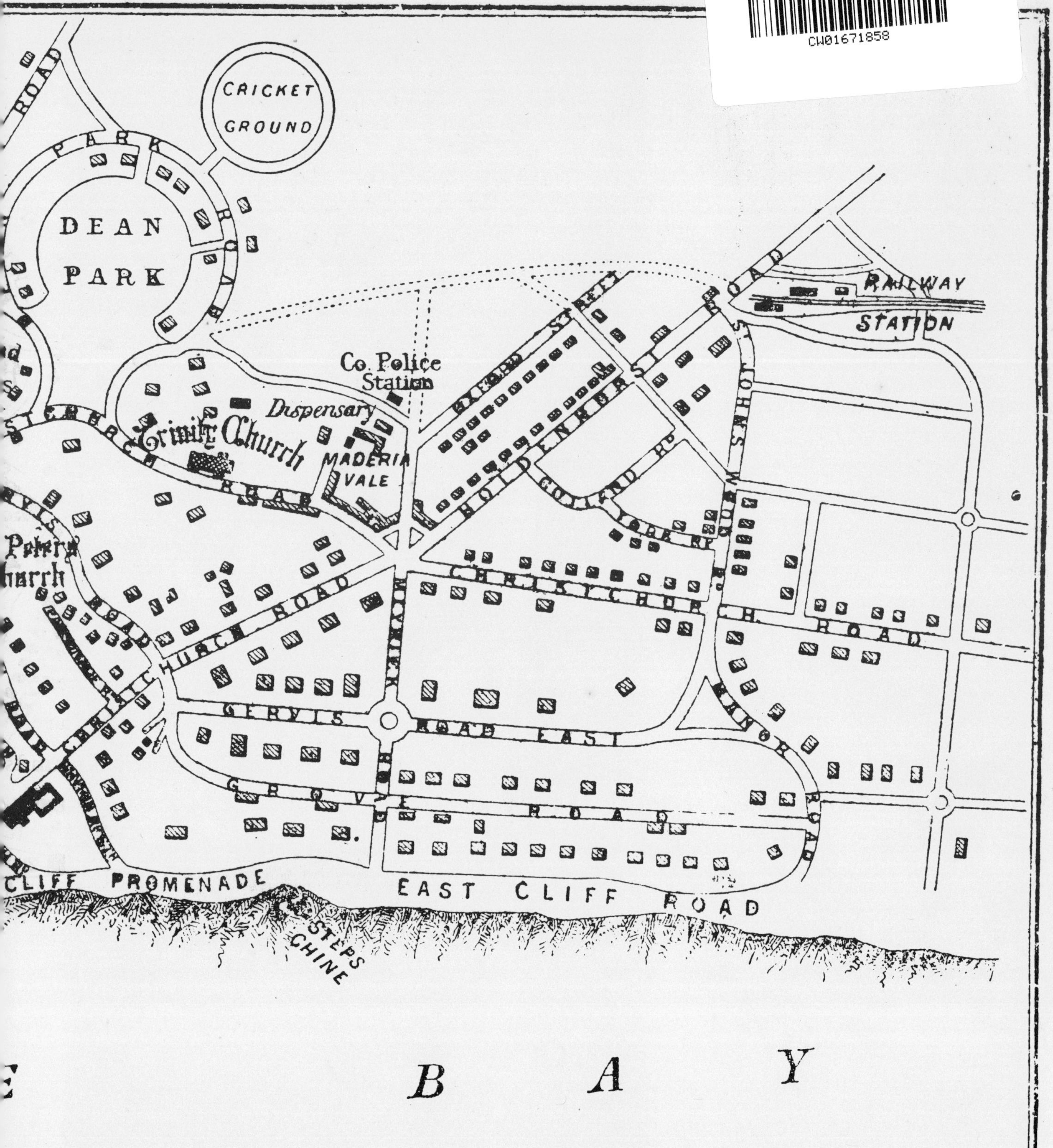
CRICKET GROUND
PARK
DEAN PARK
Co. Police Station
Dispensary
Trinity Church
MADERIA VALE
RAILWAY STATION
OXFORD STREET
CHRISTCHURCH ROAD
GERVIS ROAD EAST
GROVE ROAD
MANOR ROAD
CLIFF PROMENADE
EAST CLIFF ROAD
STEPS CHINE
B A Y

1975 **GRESHAM** 1985

Limited edition specially commissioned
to commemorate the 10th Anniversary
of Gresham's move to Bournemouth.

THE BOOK OF BOURNEMOUTH

FRONT COVER: A partly imaginary view of The Belle Vue and beach in mid-19th century, and the first landing stage, erected 1855. (DCL)

Town centre from the east in March 1980. Between Wessex Way underpass and the circular Compton House a hole was being excavated for a store and covered car-park at Richmond Gardens. Holy Trinity tower stood above the burnt-out church. (Aerial photography by Ken Hoskin of Kitchenham Ltd.)

THE BOOK OF BOURNEMOUTH

BY

DAVID & RITA POPHAM

David Popham Rita Popham

BARRACUDA BOOKS LIMITED
BUCKINGHAM, ENGLAND
MCMLXXXV

PUBLISHED BY BARRACUDA BOOKS LIMITED
BUCKINGHAM, ENGLAND
AND PRINTED BY
BUSIPRINT LIMITED
BUCKINGHAM, ENGLAND

BOUND BY
J. W. BRAITHWAITE & SONS LIMITED
WOLVERHAMPTON, ENGLAND

JACKET PRINTED BY
CHENEY & SONS LIMITED
BANBURY, OXON

PHOTOLITHOGRAPHY BY
M.R.M. GRAPHICS LIMITED
WINSLOW, ENGLAND

DISPLAY SET IN BASKERVILLE
AND TEXT SET IN 10½/12pt BASKERVILLE BY
KEY COMPOSITION
NORTHAMPTON, ENGLAND

ISBN 0 86023 219 0

Contents

Acknowledgements

A book like this is not written from memory. We are the inheritors of those who recorded events as they happened — in guide books, reports and minutes, local newspapers, diaries and letters, histories. Much more remains to be rediscovered. We are especially indebted to Michael Edgington, Reference Librarian, East Area, Dorset County Library, and the staff of Lansdowne Library.

We are grateful to many friends in the Bournemouth Teachers' Centre Local Studies Group who have given us ideas and information over the years. Its publications are a record of inspiration for many who would never have thought they could do anything useful in local studies.

Key to Caption Credits

A	Author
DCL	Dorset County Library
HRO	Hampshire Record Office

Dedication

To Jack and Nora Parsons, Joint Presidents of the Bournemouth Teachers' Centre Local Studies Group, who have encouraged us, among many others, in the study of our environment. We should not have written this book without them.

Foreword

by Cllr Frank Beale

It is an honour to be invited to write a few words of introduction and commendation to *The Book of Bournemouth.*

David and Rita Popham have written a story full of life and vivid description, with many fascinating illustrations. They have conducted immense research, and taken great pains to organise a selection from a great amount of available material.

It was in 1886 that David Popham's grandfather came to Bournemouth, transferring his fine-art business from Northampton to 170 Old Christchurch Road. It is a coincidence that my grandfather J. E. Beale had moved to Bournemouth only five years earlier to start his own business. The population at the time was under 17,000, but both men felt sure the town had a great future.

Modern Bournemouth has a history of 175 years, but much has happened in that time. This book will enable the reader to capture the spirit of the pioneers who helped to create the town, and to respect the achievement of those who followed.

This book is a tribute to all the men and women who, by imagination, innovation and sheer hard work have contributed to make Bournemouth what it is today. It is to be hoped that it will also encourage and inspire all who are now working for the good of the town and who will do so in the future.

Frank Beale

Preface

by Cllr Michael Filer, Mayor

It is not often that one has an opportunity to read a thorough in-depth history of one's own town, and having had just this chance I am delighted to be able to state what a great asset this will be to the residents of Bournemouth, and to all those who have visited or will be visiting our beautiful town.

It was not until I had the honour of being elected as Mayor of Bournemouth, and visited so many of our districts and met people active in many different walks of life, that I had the chance to appreciate what an interesting history this town has, and to have authors of the calibre of David and Rita Popham write this book is a tribute to the town as a whole.

I wish them and their book every possible success and am sure that it will provide interesting and stimulating reading for many people.

Michael Filer

Pleasure City

An outlying eastern tract of enormous Egdon Waste . . yet on the very verge of that tawny piece of antiquity such a glittering novelty as this pleasure city had chosen to spring up.

Thomas Hardy: *Tess of the D'Urbervilles*

Near this spot (Iford) a road diverges towards the south-west which leads to Poole, passing over a track of country, which a few years since, was a wild uncultivated and uninhabited area, the resort only of the illicit traffickers in contraband goods; but now brought into a state of tillage, studded with neat habitations, and with a fine level carriage road.

Historical and Descriptive Account of the town and borough of Christchurch. (1836)

The cold is so intense here, deep snow, and I can't get my rooms up to 60.

Benjamin Disraeli, at Bournemouth, 1874.

Advertisement

The frequent enquiries that have been made by the Visitors at Bournemouth, for some handbook indicating the local peculiarities and circumstances of that admired watering-place, and guiding to the principal objects of interest in neighbourhood, have induced the hasty compilation of the particulars contained in the present publication which, it is hoped, may be found useful to those for whose information it designed.

John Sydenham: *The visitor's guide to Bournemouth.* (1840)

The traveller whose love for antiquity and historic association has grown to be a ruling passion, so as to render him incapable of thoroughly enjoying scenes unstamped by the memory of deeds in the ages gone by, will find but little to interest him at Bournemouth.

Philip Brannon: *The Illustrated Historical and Picturesque Guide to Bournemouth.* (1855)

Mr George Barnes of Syracuse N.Y. came to this Hotel on crutches March 21 and was carried upstairs. This morning he walked out with perfect ease thanks to Bournemouth air and the home comforts of this Hotel. June 25 1892.

Newlyn's Royal Exeter Hotel: Visitors' Book.

ENDPAPERS: FRONT: 'New Map of Bournemouth' 1873. The Bourne Bridge is the town centre, and Christchurch Road leads from the Pier to the un-named Lansdowne. The winding roads laid out by early surveyors are conspicuous. (DCL) BACK: Bournemouth and Boscombe piers from 19th century engravings.

Introduction

When Charles Darwin saw early Bournemouth it reminded him of Patagonia. He was born the year before the first plot of building land changed hands here and, if evolution was slow to begin, we have made up time.

A century ago the shore showed a few clifftop villas, a pier and sand; two centuries ago only the sand was there, untrodden except by fisherman, smuggler or shipwrecked sailor. By the standards of a seaside resort, the bay was wasted, and the thought of such an emptiness is almost frightening.

To people from historic towns, Bournemouth must seem rootless. The only ancient building is Kinson church tower, and that has been within the town only since 1931. Parts of Stourfield House dating from 1766 make it the oldest dwelling. Between a Norman castle at Christchurch and 15th century Town Cellars at Poole, Bournemouth is as Thomas Hardy described it — 'A fair place suddenly created by the stroke of a wand, and allowed to get a little dusty'. The town's first guide-book could only praise Poole as 'remarkably clean'.

But it is easy to make fun of Bournemouth, whose very name has been a byword for primness and snobbery — or at least for comfortable idleness and enjoyment of ill-health. When Grantley Berkeley, who managed in 1865 to fill two volumes of *Life and Recollections*, stayed at Beacon Lodge, Highcliffe, Bournemouth was 'the prettiest, most pretending, but generally stupidest place I ever was in . . . I would infinitely sooner reside at little Mudeford than at overgrown Bournemouth.' The new town was accepted slowly; writers compared it with Montpelier or a German spa, its sands with Boulogne, its woods with Canada.

Bournemouth today can stand on its own reputation. Few towns have over 16% of their area as parks, gardens and recreation grounds, especially when so much of that 1,899 acres is close to the town centre. Though a seaside resort, it has kept its business centre half a mile inland from the shore, linked by lawns and pine-walks. As a town it has never built itself a town hall.

The town itself is so new that the 18th century is almost prehistory, in that hardly a document remains from that time. Few Bournemouth residents can claim to be third generation natives, and anyone here for ninety years surveys half the town's history. 'Bournemouth is a town unhampered by a past', wrote the Mayor in 1914. Some of the past fills the pages of this book.

Holdenhurst and Little Down. 1910: OS 6″ to one mile. The Wimborne road from Christchurch (now Castle Lane) runs diagonally to the still-existing lodge of Hadden's Hill. (DCL)

First Footprints

As anyone knows who tries gardening on the higher parts of Bournemouth, the soil is a coarse sand that time and cultivation have worried grey. It is a sour, hungry soil, swallowing humus and gulping rain, and almost invulnerable to flood.

To a geologist these are the Bagshot Beds, lying on this London Clay that dips south-eastward. Pockets of pipe-clay, that once fed Branksome potteries, emerge above the Bourne. Four hundred feet and more below the town lies chalk, folded westward to a ridge — the Purbeck Hills.

There fifty million years ago lay tropical uplands leading by a luxuriant valley to marshland where the bay is now. These are the Freshwater Beds; farther east vegetation dropped by long-dried rivers formed the Marine Beds. Warren Hill, the high ground of Hengistbury Head, is dark with ironstone.

The bay is new — it has taken its present form in the last ten thousand years. It was perhaps twenty million years ago that a river flowed through it eastward, its valley bounded on the farther side by a chalk ridge once joining Purbeck to Wight. Climate's long changes drained the sea, while northward-flowing rivers cut the ridge; the sea returned, felling chalk stacks between Handfast Point and the Needles. Waves now scoured the sandy cliffs to fashion the bay's smooth curve. Bournemouth today is no more than a full stop towards the end of a geological chapter, in which a few words more remain to write.

The town's gravelled uplands are terraced by changing river levels. Overlain by an urban blanket, the dry beds of streams are the town's valleys. East Common, between Charminster and Holdenhurst Roads, drained eastward across Vale Road through Boscombe Gardens to the sea. Richmond Park Road was the watershed beyond which the valley below Peter's Hill at Winton, and along Queen's Park Avenue, reached the Stour. The west cliff chines are themselves old river courses, and some still have a trace of streams. The Bourne valley itself is the largest chine.

The beach is the sea's digestion of the cliffs; since sea-walls cut off the supply of sand the beach has thinned. For thousands of years nobody complained of cliff-erosion, since none lived there. The Stour too has cut into gravel terraces at Muscliffe and Tuckton but, where the river recedes from higher terrain, its alluvium has left the only fertile ground. Though farms and market gardens still exist, that is the only area not yet developed.

Two centuries ago the beach was empty. No million footprints lay there at the end of a summer's day. The flooding tide swept away no sandcastles, but at the bay's eastern end were the Double Dykes, ramparts of an Iron Age trading and industrial settlement only recently explored. Archaeology has found traces of roads among foundations of timber round-houses built there two and a half thousand years ago. Linked with Poole Harbour and the later Roman port at Hamworthy, Hengistbury (or whatever it was called then) traded with the Continent from its now-silted harbour. Bronze and iron-working, jewellery, coins and salt-making were the industries, and traces of amphorae prove an import trade. Since most Bournemouth land was disturbed for the first time when archaeology was becoming a science, some of the finds were properly recorded and even preserved. Large-scale excavation for the railway turned up many palaeolithic flints.

A neolithic long barrow was excavated in 1936 at Holdenhurst. Bronze-Age burial urns have been found from Kinson to Iford. At Ensbury Park in 1935 pieces of daub from Iron-Age huts still showed marks of wattle and print of fingers. In 1969, outside Riviera flats on the East Cliff, road works revealed Iron-Age pottery. Roman spades left their marks on Hengistbury.

Campaigning against Alfred in 877, a Danish fleet struck on Peveril ledge, scattering its timbers on the shore. In 1407, when a whale was washed up to become the property of the Priory, a clerk scribing the Christchurch Cartulary named the spot 'la Bournemowth'. John Leland, the King's Antiquary, noted what he saw about 1540 — 'Christes-Church Twinham viij miles from Pole'. So much for Bournemouth. But in Leland's time Henry VIII's surveyor, searching for where the French might land, wrote on their map — 'Crechurche to Bowurnemouth ys vii mylys: feyer landyngs within a quarter of a myull or the lande & drawthe iiii fethum water'. Bournemouth had its first advertisement.

Against Spain in 1574 Christchurch could muster 316 men to guard the shore from Lymington to Bournemouth. When, on 3 August 1588 the Armada's alien and greedy eyes peered towards land, the cliffs were no more than a line in the haze. Admiral Blake's battle against the Dutch in February 1653 echoed from the shore. Few would have sought the glow in the sky from Wareham's fire in 1762.

The first printed advice to travellers was in 1698, when John Ogilby published his national atlas of road maps in strip form. *A Survey of the road from London to Pool* passes from Ringwood over Palmer's Bridge 'Then by (Ham)Preston-Ch, on the Right, come to Long Ham-V. at 104'1 entering Dorsetsh. and crossing a brook over Ham-Br'.

The route then lay not directly by the present road but through Kinson and up Poole Lane. 'At 104'6 pass thro Knaston-V. where an irregular R, by Hick-House (High Howe) on the Right, leads at 110'3 to Pool . . . which at present is gone much to decay.'

The 'Branch from Pool to Lemington' left the Wimbourne road by a right turn, 'when an Asc. followed by a Desc. brings you at 5'1 to Hampsh. (At 7'1 the Right to Pokesdown). Then thro Ifford-V. at 8'5 come at 10'2 to Christ-Church . . .'.

Defoe's tour in the 1720s visited Christchurch — 'a very inconsiderable poor place, scarce worth seeing, and less worth mentioning in this account . . . From here I stept up into the country north-west, to see the ancient town of Wimburn . . . South of this town over a sandy wild and barren country, we came to Pool, a considerable sea-port'. Defoe, like other travellers, avoided the future site of Bournemouth. Robert Trotman died here. For alleged smuggling he was 'barbarously Murderd on the Shore near Poole the 24 March 1765'. Kinson for his burial implies his death was on the Dorset beach.

'Cross'd much bleak, heathy country, till near Longham, where I passed a handsome river, over a long stone bridge. The road then continues over the same dreary country', wrote John Byng, later Viscount Torrington, in his 1782 *Ride into the West.* Seven years later, King George III, travelling to his first summer holiday in Weymouth, journeyed from Lyndhurst by way of Salisbury and Blandford, avoiding empty Bournemouth. But the Duke of Rutland discovered it on 4 August 1795 by chance. 'From Christchurch . . . we proceeded on horseback towards Poole. After going about two miles on the highroad, we turned off by the advice of a farmer, who told us, we should find a much shorter way by going to the left, which however would not do for a carriage. We accordingly followed his direction till we came to the top of a high cliff, where we could not find the least track of a road. We were however in some degree recompensed, by a most delightful view of the sea.'

'After enjoying this noble scene, we turned our horses' heads in order to discover some road, which we at last effected. We rode as we thought in the direction towards Poole, for on the barren uncultivated heath where we were, there was not a human being to direct us. We were not however mistaken, as after a most dreary ride, we found ourselves on the high road, from whence we looked down upon Poole, and its environs.' The poet Robert Southey was more succinct. 'On the morning of 11th September (1797), I found myself on Poole Heath, walking through desolation.' For him, staying at Burton, Poole was the place beyond Christchurch.

On 16 May 1786 the Christchurch minister buried William Collins 'who was found Dead in Poole heath' — the parish clerk adding 'who was kill'd by a Cart'. Saxton's Dorset map in 1575 named it as Sturfeld heathe, leading to Iverbridge and Holenest. To some it was Christchurch Heath or Poors Common, to others Wallis Down or Little Down, where prehistoric mounds like Maze Barrow or Fern Barrow were the only landmarks. Even the sea was unadopted, being named Poole Bay on Admiralty charts only from 1810.

'18 victims of Halsewell wrecked Purbeck 6 Jan 1786, washed up on West Shore and buried at Christchurch', records the parish register. To people of that town the West Shore was the beach beyond Hengistbury head, to the limit of their parish at the Dorset border. After a storm on 11 February 1866 '12 corpses were left on our shore' and carried to Christchurch. Up to 1843, when Highcliffe was separated, the town had eight miles of shore.

The same burial register names the only feature on the track to Poole. '23 April 1769 Mary wife of John Brian from Coy Pond . . . 15 November 1812 John Russell aged 13 months of Decoy Pond, scalded to death.' The Bourne was dammed where the track crossed, and it was used as a duck decoy.

The Salisbury and Winchester Journal mentioned the Decoy Pond House as a smugglers' resort in 1762. Potts' *Gazetteer* in 1810 and Cary's *New Itinerary* in 1819 both mention Bourn House as a landmark between Poole and Christchurch. A Malmesbury tithe survey in 1796 showed over seven acres of land there, with meadows and bee garden. The town was a decoy two centuries ago.

'Surveyed the West Coast to Flagstaff, from thence to Parkstone examined Mr Wise and signed his book in Iford and surveyed his journal for the month . . .' So reads the record of Abram Pike, Customs and Excise supervisor at Christchurch. On 2 January 1803 he rode twenty-five miles. 'West Coast' was the whole of Bournemouth Bay into Dorset as far as Canford Cliffs.

The next fortnight took him to Flagstaff again and North Haven (Sandbanks), as well as inland to Hurn and Parley on 'discoveries' — though he discovered no contraband. One day 'at Bourn, and in the Heath, found a seized 63 casks of foreign spirits and one case of tobacco'. On 4 October 'in the Heath at Bourn' he and his officers watched the warning flash of flint and steel all around them, but found no smugglers.

Abram Pike searched at Kinson and Littledown, while at 'Boskum' he knew the smugglers were waiting for a ship. On 23 February a Christchurch boatman told him of a landing there, and he seized 'two waggons and one cart with 250 casks of foreign spirits and tobacco and one case of playing cards . . . again set out with soldiers to the Bay at Boskum'. He could call for assistance from the Royal Horse Artillery at Christchurch barracks.

At Kinson church, where Robert Trotman from Wiltshire has lain since 1765 beneath his enigmatic epitaph, the tower parapet is grooved with rope-marks where (it is said) contraband was stored. A tomb near the porch is pointed out as a hiding-place. In 1770 Richard Hughes of Wick informed the authorities of a smuggling cutter in Christchurch Bay. The respectable Dr Quartley of Christchurch, who in 1805 received his share of Bournemouth's Enclosure land, related being called out at night by two muffled men to extract a musket-ball from a smuggler — who reminded him of the incident fifteen years later.

But the legendary Bournemouth smuggler was Isaac Gulliver, born at Semington, near Trowbridge, in 1745. Stories are told of his fifty men in livery and powdered wigs, and his trains of contraband that stretched two miles across the heath. Gulliver lived at Howe Lodge in Kinson, and in West Borough, Wimborne. His daughter married a Wimborne banker, William Fryer, and he was buried, a respectable citizen, in the Minster in 1822.

The third Earl of Malmesbury, born in 1807, recalled in his boyhood watching smugglers hiding kegs of brandy in his father's park and being rewarded with one for his silence. He related a family story that about 1780 the Earl of Shaftesbury, visiting Hurn Court, was amazed to see waggons loaded with kegs clatter past. His host ignored them, and a detachment of cavalry found no-one who could tell them the smugglers' direction.

The great heath which became Bournemouth belonged to a small settlement on the west bank of the Stour. Three miles from Christchurch, of which it was a chapelry, Holdenhurst was an outpost of that town, a colony clinging to the narrow strip of fertile meadows that stretched inland towards the next river town, Wimborne. In 1808, when the ancient Holdenhurst chapel was promoted to parish church of the vast area then enclosed, scarcely a cottage broke the barren heath towards the Dorset border four miles westward.

Holdenhurst had eight centuries of history before Bournemouth Commissioners' District numbered two thousand people. Domesday gives it as Holeest; in Baldwin de Revers charter about 1162 it is Holeherest; on the first Hampshire map in Saxton's county atlas it is Holensesse — the wood of the holly or holm-oak. 'A garden of hyves' there was left in John Howkie's will of 1560 who, like John Hokee of Mukylshill in 1588 and John Corbin of Holnhurst in 1590, left money to the village chapel, the parish church and Iford Bridge. At the dissolution of Christchurch Priory in 1539 the Vicar was allowed £26 for ministers there and one at Holdenhurst chapel, where were 'nine score houseling people' — those who received Communion.

The site of Bournemouth was the riverside village. The Bourne valley was Holdenhurst Bottom, and the first bridge across it was still known as Holdenhurst Bridge in 1856. In 1722 and 1735 the Overseers paid for repairs to the road at Boorn, and in 1743 Boorne Plank was mended. Past that place, the *Hampshire Directory* advised in 1784 'Henry Reeks waggon goes to Poole, Monday and Thursday, and returns each Night'. The first Ordnance Survey map shows the Decoy House just above the 'plank' where the track crossed — now the site of the Square.

From Holdenhurst the road to Poole led past Townsend and near to the settlement of Great Dean; the present Queens Park Avenue was Great Dean Bottom. The long valley, where traffic now climbs Wessex Way, was Longman's Bottom. From Strouden Pond a stream flowed along Shiphouse Lane (now Woodbury Avenue) to Eel Pond, turning north along Throop Lane to Holdenhurst village street, whence it drained through river meadows to the Stour. Until the 1920s many cottages there had footbridges. Another stream flowed across the road to a large clear pool at Longmoor Lane — now Riverside Avenue. The poorhouse was south-west of the surviving Townsend Cottages, and the overseers in 1813 remarked on its unhealthy site. Empty land at Strouden was swampy forty years ago.

Almost a mile up the Stour from Holdenhurst church is Throop, spelt as Drup in Christchurch baptism register in 1742. Robert Bound was maltster and cooper in 1776, and John Cutlar shoemaker there in 1699. At Muccleshell in 1702 the inventory of Richard Sleate's property showed £60 worth in his clothier's shop. Once the Hall, Muccleshell Farm shows some timber-framing, and Muscliffe Farm is still a substantial house. All those settlements ran parallel to the Stour, through which were fords to the east bank — Pigshoot at the end of Yeoman's Lane, and Blackwater. The Enclosure Award shows the Jolly Sailor alehouse opposite Throop Mill, whose flour was used for a ship's biscuit bakery nearby. In the 18th century a tannery was at Muscliffe.

Many of the Holdenhurst names are common in the town today — Corbin, Hockey and Reeks. The Enclosure Award lists 132 people, of whom nine were Troke. Though the Dean family held parish office forty-five times from 1688 to 1826, as 'substantial house-holders . . . ancient inhabitants', Troke can be taken as the characteristic Bournemouth name.

High ground between Holdenhurst and the Bourne was Littledown; until the 1920s it was grazed by sheep, which were driven through Sheepwash above Iford Bridge. At the same date Broadway Lane was still a narrow track, while Muscliffe Lane is only now being progressively widened as new roads to housing estates lead from it. Moordown a mile south was described by Morden Bennett, appealing in 1853 for St John's school chapel, as still 'a tract of heath-land on which many poor families are settled'. The names of Hookey and Corben are in a notice to quit Moordown Farm in 1787.

For the people of Holdenhurst then, the heath was theirs. They would walk to the mouth of the Bourne to help haul in the nets for the reward of a few mackerel. The young men of William West's farm escaped a press-gang there one evening in 1803, running back to Muscliffe over their familiar heath. *Sydenham's Guide* in 1840 describes 'the drawing of the seines (for mackerel and herring) especially on moonlight evenings, producing a remarkable effect'.

Townsend Cottages at Holdenhurst have given their name to the town's newest estate. This photograph is taken from the footbridge over the A338, which has cut the road past the cottages. (A)

ABOVE: Iford bridge. Downstream arches (left) are rebuilding of 1784, the others copied in 1934 when a new bridge opened and the old one closed to motor traffic. (A) CENTRE: Holdenhurst church on its 150th anniversary service, June 1984; the old church was on the north. (A) BELOW: New House (late 18th century) probably built for William Clapcott. The thatched Old House beyond is 17th century. (A) RIGHT: Built in 1793, Pelhams was later Kinson vicarage and is now the community centre. (A)

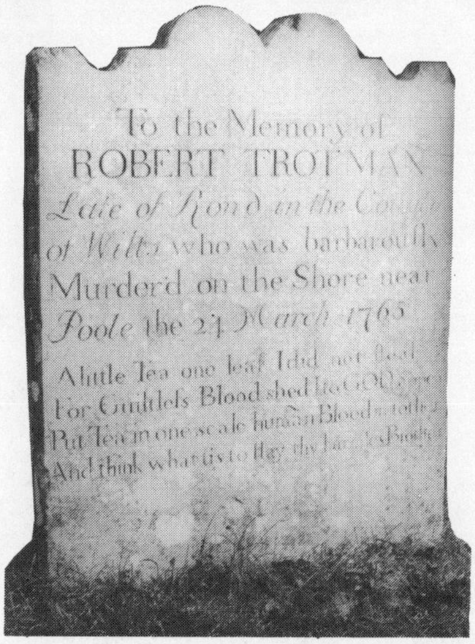

ABOVE: Contraband concealed in tower and tomb is the gnarled history of Kinson church. (A) LEFT: Headstone at Kinson of an alleged smuggler. (A) RIGHT: This plaque on a brick pillar stands near St John's church.

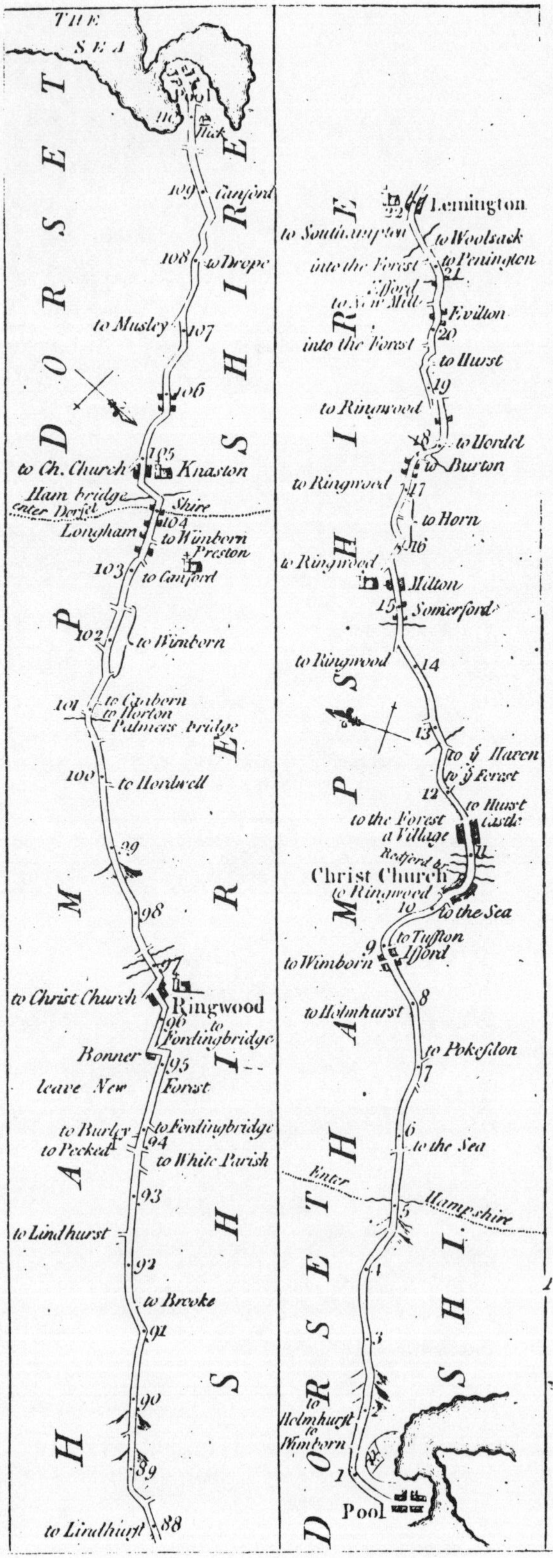
THE SEA
DORSETSHIRE
HAMPSHIRE
Pool
Canford
to Drope
to Musley
to Ch. Church
Knaston
Ham bridge
Shire
enter Dorset
Longham
to Wimborn
Preston
to Canford
to Wimborn
to Cranborn
to Horton
Palmers bridge
to Horbwell
to Christ Church
Ringwood
to Fordingbridge
Bonner
leave New Forest
to Burley
to Fordingbridge
to Pecked
to White Parish
to Lindhurst
to Brooke
to Lindhurst
Lemington
to Southampton
to Woolsack
into the Forest
to Penington
to New Mill
Evilton
into the Forest
to Hurst
to Ringwood
to Hordel
Burton
to Ringwood
to Horn
to Ringwood
Milton
Somerford
to Ringwood
to y Haven
to y Forest
to Hurst Castle
to the Forest
a Village
Christ Church
to Ringwood
to the Sea
to Tuffton
Ifford
to Wimborn
to Holmhurst
to Pokesdon
to the Sea
Enter Hampshire
to Holmhurst
to Wimborn
Pool

TO THE MEMORY OF
LEWIS D. G. TREGONWELL
WHO ERECTED THE FIRST HOUSE
IN BOURNEMOUTH ON THIS SITE IN 1810.
HE DIED ON JAN. 18TH 1832, AGED 73.
AND WAS BURIED IN
ST. PETER'S CHURCHYARD, BOURNEMOUTH.
HE WAS DESCENDED FROM SIR JOHN TREGONWELL
A MEMBER OF AN ANCIENT CORNISH FAMILY.
THIS TABLET IS ERECTED BY MEMBERS OF THE
BOURNEMOUTH AND DISTRICT CORNISH
ASSOCIATION AND FRIENDS, OCT. 1937.

TREGONWELL ARMS
WINES
SPIRITS
AND
BASS
ALES

OPPOSITE LEFT: Part of John Ogilby's road atlas of 1698. (HRO) ABOVE: Commemorative plaque on the Royal Exeter Hotel. (A) CENTRE: The name of C. R. Hayball dates this picture to the last years of Bournemouth's first inn, opened in 1809 as the Tapps Arms. Closed in 1883, the building survived under two years. It stood back from Old Christchurch Road at Post Office Road. (DCL) BELOW: Charminster Road, about 1900. (DCL) ABOVE: Redhill Ferry crossed the Stour from the nearer side to West Parley, whose farmers were able to have it closed in 1934. For many years the Lawfords, then their daughter's family the Marshalls operated both ferry and tea-gardens. (DCL) BELOW: Iford, seen from the Christchurch side, across the Stour, was a village until this century. (DCL)

ABOVE: Wick Ferry was a link from Tuckton to Christchurch by 1800, close to a ford. The land beyond is Quomps, where Pontin's holiday camp now stands and still operates a seasonal crossing. (DCL)
BELOW: The road at Throop Mill, in a watercolour of the 1940s by Kathleen M. Chilver. (DCL)

ABOVE: The old church at Holdenhurst was pulled down when the present church opened in 1834, and its masonry used in cottages nearby. (L) BELOW: Muscliff Farm in a watercolour by Kathleen M. Chilver. (DCL)

ABOVE: This 1887 view from the Mont Dore shows Richmond Hill Congregational Church as it existed 1859-91, when the present church replaced it. (DCL) BELOW: 1893. Blackwater Ferry was named after the hamlet on the Hurn side of the Stour, where this ferryman's house stood. Access was by Church Lane at Holdenhurst. (DCL)

Villas and Visions

As last century began, the face of Bournemouth bore scarcely a man-made feature. When most of it was unmarked heath, parishes nearby in Dorset and Hampshire had been communities for a thousand years. In the 18th century the nature of those villages had been changed by private enclosure acts dividing the common and waste into hedged fields, to which new straight roads gave access. Encouraged by demands for more efficient agriculture in the wars against France, Parliament in 1801 passed a General Enclosure Act, making it much simpler to divide parish commons and waste among local landowners and others who would pay for it.

They lost no time, and next year a private Act became law 'for dividing, allotting and inclosing certain Commonable Lands and Waste Grounds within the Parish or Chapelry of Holdenhurst in the County of Southampton'. Three years later, in 1805, the three Commissioners appointed by the Act made their Award — a book of ninety-one large parchment sheets.

The Award (which covered also Hurn, Winkton and Hinton Admiral — all outside Bournemouth) divided up the Liberty of Westover. This area was eventually most of the County Borough before the 1931 acquisitions from Dorset. Just over half the 5,084 acres was allocated to the forty-one owners of common rights in the Liberty in return for their loss. The tithes payable to the Earl of Malmesbury on all land in the Liberty was compensated by 316 acres, reckoned as an eighth of the area remaining. As owner of his 'Rights and Interests in and to the soil', Sir George Tapps was given 240 acres, about 4.7% of all land in the Award. Roads, mostly forty feet wide, accounted for 78 acres, (1.5%) and small areas were set aside for gravel and clay digging. But important to the town's future was the 425 acres in five scattered allotments, held in trust by Sir George Tapps as Lord of the Manor for cottagers 'in Lieu of their Rights or pretended Rights or customs of cutting Turves' for fuel — a grant of turbary.

However, it was the seven purchasers of land in the Liberty of Westover who benefitted most. Before an Award was made, its administration had to be paid for, and the three Commissioners estimated that sale of 1,258 acres, about a quarter of the land in the Liberty of Westover, would be sufficient. It was auctioned in twenty-seven lots and raised £4,100.

As might be expected, Sir George Tapps himself was interested, buying 205 acres, rather less than he had gained from compensation. The Earl of Malmesbury, already allocated 316 acres, bought only sixty more. But the great beneficiary from the sale was William Dean of the mansion on Little Down, who not only bought 500 acres (40% of the land sold), but paid less per acre than any other purchaser. Land in Bournemouth sold then for twenty-five shillings an acre.

Not only was the area important but so was the location of land. The Earl of Malmesbury's four lots were mostly in Moordown and Strouden, but he paid some £28 an acre for meadow land near Iford Bridge. By contrast, Sir George Tapps' 205 acres from the Bourne towards Boscombe cost £5 an acre. With more land on the East Cliff and in Southbourne he now owned most of the sea-front. William Dean's four cheap lots from the cliff-top west of the Bourne to Alum Chine, and northward to the Poole Road, gave him over 400 acres of potentially valuable land. Part of the future King's Park near his house also became his property.

Though the remaining four purchasers did not have Dean's foresight or his connections, (one of the three Commissioners, William Clapcott, was his son-in-law and became his heir in 1812), their payments were not wasted. Two had no established interests in the Liberty of Westover. Arthur Quartley was a Christchurch doctor and several times Mayor, buying a 21-acre lot in the present Stokewood Road area. William Driver was a south London speculator who bought an eighth of the land sold, mostly near the future Meyrick Park. His 16 acres in Moordown he exchanged for much more in Branksome with Rev G. T. Brice, Vicar of Great Canford, who already farmed between Redhill and the Stour.

Finally, two local owners, Philip Norris of Boscombe Cottage, and Cornelius Trim, who farmed at Muccleshell and Throop, bought smaller areas. Holdenhurst parish records mention a seventeenth-century Cornelius Trim as churchwarden and overseer.

By 1 May 1807 all land purchased had to be enclosed by a fence which 'forever afterwards shall be well and sufficiently maintained supported and kept in repair'. If adjoining a road or parish boundary, the land had to be fenced at once. The Commissioners approved four exchanges among purchasers. The most important was three acres of the Earl of Malmesbury's Lot 128 at Throop, given for three of Sir George Tapps' Lot 31 at Bourne Mouth, so giving the Earl a plot of land by the sea.

The Earl of Malmesbury was concerned with the Award more as it related to the Manor of Hurn. As James Harris, he had been created Baron Malmesbury in 1788 for his work as a diplomat, becoming Viscount Fitzharris and Earl of Malmesbury in 1800. His son, who succeeded in 1820, developed the estate, rebuilding much of the house whose name he soon changed to Heron Court. The third Earl published his reminiscences as a diplomat, the estate passing to his nephew, the fourth Earl. In 1899 his son James Edward succeeded but, on his death in 1950, the family left the house, whose name he had changed back to Hurn Court fifteen years before. Since 1952 it has been a private school, five minutes' walk outside Bournemouth by a private bridge over the Stour.

The Manor of Christchurch, bought by Sir Peter Mews in 1708, was inherited by his cousin George Ivison Tapps seventy years later. Becoming first Baronet in 1791, he left the Manor and the Hinton Admiral estates to his son George William, who added the name Gervis, from George Jarvis, Sir Peter Mews' father-in-law.

At the second Baronet's death in 1842 the Manor was held in trust for his son, George Eliott Tapps-Gervis, then aged fifteen, who inherited the Meyrick estates in Anglesey through his wife. Since 1876 the family has been Tapps-Gervis-Meyrick, and the sixth Baronet, owner of Bournemouth estates today, is descended directly from the Lord of the Manor at the time of the Enclosure Award.

John Dean had built a house at Little Down inherited by William, who left it to his son-in-law William Clapcott, one of the Enclosure Commissioners. In turn the estate passed in 1833 to his son William Clapcott Dean, and in 1887 to a relative, John Edward Cooper, who had married Elizabeth Dean. Adopting the name of Cooper-Dean he took great interest in the town's development, and lived to be 81. Joseph Cooper-Dean was the owner from 1921 to 1950, and the death of his second daughter on 14 April 1984 ended more than two centuries of the family at Littledown.

The great heath which existed as the nineteenth century dawned was now, in 1805, marked with roads and divided among landowners. But being mostly heath, little of the 5,084 acres of the Award was developed for agriculture. It awaited another destiny.

'I have one remark to make: that if a man has made a great alteration in the appearance of the country, and of my native place, he has robbed it of its greatest beauties . . . When I look back to the beginning of this century, when the wide extent of many thousand acres was clothed with the beautiful heather . . . I can hardly feel that the world is progressing, but retrograding in these days.'

Writing in 1871 at Tuckton, farmer Richard Dale did not live in the most altered part of the area. 'The bee garden was by the side of the common from Wick to Wimborne . . .' He was writing of what was then called Wimborne Road, once joining the religious houses of Wimborne and Christchurch. The Enclosure Commissioners made this track above the Stour flood-plain into one of their four main roads. Later it was known as Strouden Lane, and in this century as Castle Lane — perhaps referring to Christchurch castle.

The road 'from Decoy Pond Cottage to Bourn Mouth' has become Exeter Road; and another led from Poole Road to Boscombe Chine. The fourth track, 'from Redhill to Coombe Corner' climbed from the Stour crossing towards the present Ensbury Park area.

But it was the main roads the Commissioners created that are most conspicuous on later maps. From where the Poole to Christchurch route crossed the Bourne half a mile inland, a new straight road climbed the hill to strike northward. After another half-mile it branched at a point long called Rush Corner (now Cemetery Junction), left past Maze Barrow and turning towards Redhill, right and less directly to Throop. Holdenhurst was reached better by a branch from the Christchurch road at the point later known as the Lansdowne. The present Bath Road was once the Christchurch road from Bourne Mouth.

By such ways, between ditches and banks or 'other good and sufficient fences', Lewis Dymock Grosvenor Tregonwell and his wife drove to Bourne Chine on 14 July 1810. Over ten years before, Captain Tregonwell of the Dorset Rangers had been responsible for the farthest eastern coast of that county. His home was at Cranborne Lodge, ten miles north of Wimborne and, during a summer stay at Muddiford, he had driven over to see Bourne Mouth again.

Almost three hundred years earlier the family had come to Dorset from Manaccan in Cornwall, when John Tregonwell, as one of the King's Commissioners, had received the surrender of Milton Abbey, and bought its estates for £1,000. Now his descendant thought of a new estate at Bourne, and was able, at the age of fifty-two, to buy land from Sir George Tapps. Lewis Tregonwell married twice, acquiring much property each time; Henrietta, his second wife, was the daughter of Henry William Portman of Bryanston, near Blandford.

This first Bournemouth house-holder paid £179 10s for eight and a half acres adjoining Exeter Road between the Decoy Pond and the sea. The value of land in Bourne was climbing already. For this favoured site, sloping to the sea, that Sir George Tapps had bought for an average of £5 an acre, Tregonwell now paid £21; when only two years later he bought more, it cost £40 an acre, and still more to the west was £60 by 1822.

The mansion, named Exeter House, when leased to the Marchioness of Exeter about 1820, was the centre of an estate the family called Bourne Tregonwell. A thatched cottage built for his butler Symes remained as a relic of the old estate to 1922 when it was burnt, and though rebuilt was soon demolished for a 'bus station site. Henrietta Tregonwell lived at Portman Lodge, named after her father's family, as a widow from 1832 to her death in 1846. Another cottage, on high ground west of the mansion known as Prospect Mount, later renamed Terrace Mount, was built for the estate gardener, but also became a family residence. Its site is now the Merville Hotel in Exeter Road.

A plan of the estate dated 1835 shows Tregonwell land extending to Richmond Hill, Old Christchurch Road and Yelverton Road. The only older building was the inn of 1809 built by Sir George Tapps. Named after the new owner, it was advertised in 1837 as 'on the Turnpike Road from Poole to Christchurch . . . now used as an Inn or public house commonly called or known by the name of the Tregonwell Arms . . . at Bourne now in the occupation of the said George Fox' — who paid £30 yearly on a fourteen year lease. In 1840 he bought the inn for £600.

'In 1826 I shot an old blackcock on the very spot where St Peter's Church at Bournemouth now stands', wrote the third Earl of Malmesbury in his memoirs. The blackcock or black grouse was known also as the heath-poult, the old name of the public house at the corner of Heath Poult (now St Paul's) Road. The Earl was a keen preserver of wild life. 'Every variety of British bird', he wrote, 'even the rarest, is in the small museum at Heron Court, all having been killed within five miles of my house.'

Thirty years after the Enclosure Award, Sir George Ivison Tapps was succeeded by his son George William, who added the surname of Gervis. While MP for Christchurch from 1832 to 1837 he engaged the architect Benjamin Ferrey in 1836 to plan a 'marine village'.

Ferrey designed the town centre with a 'Pleasure Gardens Pagoda' near the sea and the row of sixteen Westover Villas to his own house-plans. To keep them exclusive they had to cost at least £500. It would have been Ferrey's plan that Dr Granville saw in 1841 as making Bournemouth 'one of twenty watering-places, just as tolerable and common'. Decimus Burton succeeded Ferrey, but Sir G. W. Tapps-Gervis died in 1842, having done in seven years more than anyone else to establish the town.

His work was carried on by trustees administering £5,000 on the planned improvements. Burton's report to the trustees in 1845 noted that 'houses of a large scale are particularly enquired for', while 'in designing a building plan for Bournemouth, formality should be carefully avoided'. He realised the attraction of the Bourne's value to a marine village, advising that in making walks and drives, tree thinning should be cautious. 'The characteristic which distinguishes Bournemouth from other watering places is its rusticity.'

More than any landowner, builder or guide-book writer, it was Dr Granville who influenced the town's development. Born in Milan in 1783 as Augustus Bozzi, he took his maternal grandmother's name and was already an authority through his book *The Spas of England* when he came almost accidentally in 1841. 'I did not learn from anyone . . . aught of the existence of the incipient living colony of that place.'

Two days revealed 'a perfect discovery among sea-nooks' . . . 'a place suitable for the resort of the better classes of society'. He admired much: 'the various structures, including the old English, the Lombard and campaniled forms, as well as the Swiss cottage', and 'still more pretending, larger and first-rate mansions built by Mr Gordon'. He warned 'If the proprietor [Mrs Tregonwell] of this blessed region is properly advised, instead of parting to speculating purchasers with her lord's estate . . . she will apply herself to build insulated villas of different sizes, and properly located with gardens . . .'. He questioned 'Look around, and interrogate vegetation at this period of the winter'. He compared: 'a real Montpelier on the south coast of England'.

Above all, he influenced. It was Granville who prophesied the future pleasure gardens, which he named Bournemouth Park — 'a regular promenade all the way, with parterres and beds of flowers'. He realised that the 'present insignificant wooden bridge . . . ought to be replaced by a handsome stone one'. He disapproved of Ferrey's plan for the Marine Village. The worst feature was 'crowning the whole with a Gothic church, placed in the middle of the summit, like a diadem — to serve as a beacon to mariners; but it will not do for invalids with delicate chests and damaged lungs to climb up the Capitol . . . to be blown away in attempting to reach the House of God, or blown upon on coming out of it by the boisterous south-wester . . .' Granville could even change geography: the coastal site, 'instead of being called Poole Bay, ought henceforth to be called Bourne Bay . . .'.

'The path becomes . . . totally unfit for ladies', the *Guide* in 1855 warned foolhardy visitors to Durley Chine. Among Bournemouth's roads wound a maze of footpaths. In 1855 Brannon was already warning against 'the mere eagerness of land selling' that threatened them. The East Cliff Pathway then was 'soon lost amongst rugged and changing sand-hills, which continue to Boscombe mouth'. The Western Plantations led past the Coastguard Station to Prospect Mount 'marked by a little mound and flagstaff'.

Brannon regretted that the way up the Marbarrow Valley, (now Meyrick Park) was closed near the Sanatorium, and hoped that Miss Talbot would 'improve and adorn . . . and conduct and open it'. A quarter of a century later this had been done, the same writer recommending the Marbarrow Valley to botanists; but paths on the common between Wimborne and Holdenhurst road were then being stopped by building.

Many were the local names for coastal features; almost any cliff fall site could be named a 'chine'. The earlier *Guide* mentions Rickes' and Watering Chine, as the coastguards called them. By 1880 Little Durley Chine led down Joseph's Steps (built by Joseph Cutler from timbers of the wrecked pier) to Durley Cove. The sea wall has smothered Durley Cove, leaving what the *Guide* called Great Durley Chine. Middle Chine was 'a very pretty passage of scenery', and Alum Chine, the largest, divided into branches towards the county border.

East of Bourne Chine itself 'bunny' is more used; the county border since 1974 has reached the coast at Chewton Bunny beyond Highcliffe. Chines have been Bournemouth itself since early days. In summer Alum Chine is the shaded humid pathway to the sea for thousands of visitors; on a winter's afternoon it is a dark, damp, green glade where a Victorian ghost would pass unnoticed.

In the middle of last century the town was earning its first street names. Brannon's town of his 1855 *Guide* named the way from the Bourne towards Christchurch as North Road, with Exeter Lane passing over the lower meadows to the shore. From there Bath Road led only as far as the hotel, with Christchurch Road beyond, where Hinton and Alma (now Upper Hinton) Roads branched off. Cliff Road (now Russell-Cotes Road) was opposite. Boscombe Grove began at the top of the hill in what is now Grove Road.

At the Bridge the road leading to Redhill had been 'formerly called by the country people Nurse's Hill or Nurse Hill'. Richmond Terrace was a row of houses on its western side, with a semi-circular drive in front. The first directory in 1859 mentions it, with West Hill and Commercial Road — the only business street name that has survived to the present day. Two dozen premises gave that address. Here were laundress, builder and cabinet-maker, fishmonger and upholsterer. Blacklock the chemist was there into this century, but no-one listed as a 'private resident' gave a Commercial Road address.

The present day Bourne Avenue was Sanatorium Road after that building opened in 1855, but Brannon called it Bourne Valley Road. As explained in his *Guide*, 'the right branch turns beyond the Sanatorium . . . enters the Wimborne road just beyond Richmond Terrace'. In fact he is here describing the present St Stephen's Road (where the church was begun in 1881). Brannon continues: 'This will we suppose be called the Marbarrow Road, crossing the Vale of Marbarrow'.

This name has disappeared from modern Bournemouth, but evidently referred to the valley which now runs along Braidley Road and through Meyrick Park to the railway. The first Ordnance Survey draft shows Maze Barrow a mile and a half north of the present Square, and Brannon's own map shows 'Marbarrow Valley' across the 'common turbary' of Meyrick Park. Otherwise the name is forgotten.

From a pond in Horseshoe Common a stream ran along what is now Fir Vale Road to a ravine twenty feet deep. It was known as Church Glen by 1855 and described as 'a deep dingle . . . crossed by a rustic bridge of rough fir poles'. (It is a coincidence that a shop nearby is called Dingle's). The public paid ½d toll to use the bridge which Thomas Shettle had built in 1851 for his tenants in Old Christchurch Road.

In 1866 Henry Joy began his Arcade on the site of the bridge, leaving the shops with ready-made basements. Church Glen Road in 1855 was 'a fine drive, just completed', and later renamed St Peter's Road.

'To be let, (Furnished), at eight guineas a week, A MANSION, the property of a Lady, and suitable for a Family of distinction . . . A Kitchen Garden and Two Cows can be rented, which belong to the Premises . . .'

Mrs Tregonwell's house was advertised in the *Salisbury and Winchester Journal* of 16 September 1839. Twelve years later the family's agent William Rebbeck opened the first office for land and houses. In 1890 Rebbeck's advertised 78 sites around Wickham Road, 36 of them in Christchurch Road, to be auctioned from a marquee on the ground.

The Boscombe Spa Estate sale in 1892 was for 87 plots of building land both sides of Sea Road; pencilled into a catalogue are annual rentals of the 999-year leases — £12 2s 6d to £20 10s for a corner plot. The same year 38 plots of the Tower estate were sold with frontage to Palmerston Road; it included Church Road (now St Clement's Road), and the recreation ground then called Gower Gardens — now a public open space whose original name seems to be lost.

Rebbeck's in 1892 sold the Alum Chine and Alumhurst estates, with forty-three marine building sites on 999-year leases, already laid west of the Chine from Beaulieu Road to the cliff, where Alumdale Road began a public drive to the sea. Four years later Dene Wood at the head of the Chine was advertised, with gardens of two acres and twelve freehold plots.

At Winton in 1893 the Christchurch Land Society announced the sale of Hicks Common estate, between York Road (now Green Road) and Portland Road. For '66 excellent villa sites and 12 conveniently situated shop fronts', the public could pay £1 per lot in a ballot to be held in the New Schools at the late hour of 8.30 pm.

At Southbourne the Stourcliff Estate in 1859 was being laid out by Creeke for villas. 'It will besides serve to connect Bournemouth, by a succession of polished mansions and private grounds, with the magnificent seats in the vales of Stour and Avon . . .'. The grounds of Stourfield House itself were by 1893 laid out with roads and being divided into plots. The Stourfield Park Estate lay between Stourvale, Irving, Cranleigh and Southbourne Roads. The plan shows 'proposed pleasure grounds' in the middle, but commercial pressures filled them with the houses of Stamford Road.

A mile of cliff-top with 89 acres of the original 230 that Dr Compton had bought, were in 1901 sold with the Southcliff Hotel. Ten years later Fox and Sons advertised the Stourcliffe Estate, including Stourcliffe and Pine Avenues and Bay View Road, (now part of the overcliff drive), in 64 lots. It was 'in a bracing and healthy part of Bournemouth, and is so well known that much detail in these particulars is quite unnecessary.'

Many working-people lived in Springbourne and Winton, since rents were too high in the town centre. When the West station opened in 1874, 'difficulties of lodging accommodation lead many men to walk back and forth from Poole to Bournemouth . . . wearing themselves out . . . consuming much valuable time'. When trams were discussed in 1898, Winton parish council agreed to them if half-fares were charged in early morning and evening.

Houses in the Malmesbury Park area were auctioned in 1910, when tenants in Shelbourne Road paid 7s 6d a week. At Winton the same rent was charged in Green Road, but houses in

Parker Road were 8s, being detached. At Moordown in the 1890s cottages were built for £240, and let for 4s 6d a week. When the town's Chief Sanitary Inspector retired in 1917 he looked back over thirty years in the department. 'It is now the rule, and not the exception, to find two working-class families residing in a house containing five or six rooms, and the average rent, for this class of house has increased from 5s to 10s per week.' The last ten years had seen over a thousand cases of diphtheria.

Ensbury Farm in 1916 was advertised for market gardening as well as its building potential. Lot 4, the farmhouse itself, had 'the Magnificent Frontage of about 910 feet to the Main Wimborne Road', while lots 1 and 2 totalling 42 acres had over 2,000 feet fronting Hill View Road. Agents Duke and Abbott claimed that the 88 acres of Ensbury Farm were 'Ripe for Immediate Development', though then outside the town. At Moordown the Mayfield Park Estate, advertised by the South Coast Land Society in 1912, had roads named topically King Edward, King George, Queen Mary and Coronation Avenues. Land sold to the Council became the greens and courts of Malvern Road recreation ground. In house agents' jargon the estate is now 'the Royal Avenues', and Northbourne is a name that seems little more than fifty years old.

Bright's *Guide* in 1888 was candid about Springbourne — perhaps to assure its readers that any other part of the town was better. 'The houses which are every day becoming more numerous have been erected without any pretentions to beauty.' Malmesbury Park, developed a few years later, was 'a little colony to the north-west of Springbourne, but they are far more attractive than those of the locality last described'. In the same year a guide published by the Town's Interest Association promised visitors that 'all dreary spaces are now covered with palaces in terra-cotta . . . The very roads speak of quiet and refinement, and everything is beautiful in its place'. The designer William Morris called them 'blackguard villas'.

'The laying out of a District or Colony for certain of the working classes whose work lies near the centre of the Borough', was recommended to the Council in 1917. 'Provision of suitable dwellings for the artisan, shop assistants and clerical classes will have to be faced . . .' The area specified was Mannington Place, swept from the map in the 1960s when its hundred-year-old houses were demolished for a car park.

Between the wars, outlying parts of the town were built up, made convenient by cars. Broad roads spread beyond Meyrick Park to the county border, lined with tudored houses in broad gardens. In West Way, a 40-foot road between newly-planted borders, plots 200 feet deep sold for £200. The Strouden Park and Broadway Hotels in Castle Lane were both granted licences in 1932, when the thatched Bear Cross public house was rebuilt.

In the 1930s huge blocks of flats appeared. On the hilltop above the Pavilion, Bath Hill Court in 1936 covered the site of the old St Peter's parsonage garden, and bordered Bath Road. On a similar site at Boscombe rose San Remo Towers, of foreign name and style. A quarter-century later, multi-storey flats climbed on the cliffs — Tower Court in West Cliff Road (1961-62), Admiral's Walk nearby and the Albany in Manor Road (both 1962-64). They stand on the skyline seen from Cranborne Chase, near Lewis Tregonwell's home of two centuries ago.

At the same time the town has changed more subtly. In Lansdowne and Wimborne Roads one Victorian villa after another is pulled down, to be replaced by convenient flats. Yet between those roads, on the Dean Park estate, little has changed. Behind the Holy Trinity site, the century-old villas are offices.

In 1869 Muscliffe was 'in contemplation to lay out villas for the purpose of fresh-water fishing'. A postman delivering there earned a shilling a week extra. At present the town's advance is most obtrusive in Muscliffe Lane — Bournemouth still has lanes — where broad tarmac rolls towards the Stour. Land between the river and Castle Lane was once planned as 'white' — free from development. The Hampshire Centre, Yeoman's Road industrial estate, and housing have invaded it. The Townsend estate, once the farthest point of Holdenhurst village, is now the end of Bournemouth.

ABOVE: The Bourne flows from a culvert under the Square to another below the pier. Children's Corner in the Lower Pleasure Grounds was popular between the wars. BELOW: The Lansdowne, from the Queen's Hotel, when Christchurch Road was still lined with villas. (Both DCL)

ABOVE: Across the Pleasure Grounds in 1863, Southbourne Terrace was still incomplete. At left is the 'Scotch' church at the foot of CENTRE: Richmond Hill, here on a sunny morning about 1880. BELOW: The bridge over the Bourne at the Pier Approach, showing the Pleasure Grounds in the 1870s. (All DCL)

OPPOSITE LEFT: 1865: Terrace Cottage stands above Exeter Road, built by Tregonwell for his gardener, but later used for the family. RIGHT: On Boscombe Hill c1862. CENTRE: Westover Road and Bath Hotel in 1840, two years after completion. BELOW: The view from Terrace Mount in 1842 shows Old Christchurch Road, Gervis Place, the year-old St Peter's, Westover Villas and the Bath Hotel. ABOVE: The 'Scotch' church and Southbourne Terrace in 1875. BELOW: J. Newman's 1855 engraving shows St Peter's Church complete, though the tower was built in 1869 and the spire ten years later. (All DCL)

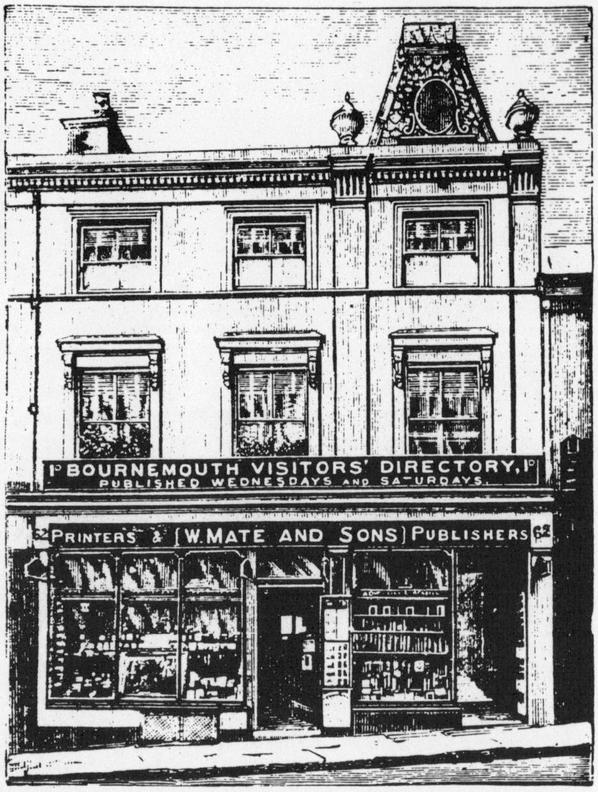

LEFT: Portman Lodge, built 1811 for his butler, Symes, by Lewis Tregonwell, whose widow died there in 1846. Burnt down in 1922. The spire is St Andrew's. (DCL) RIGHT: William Mate, whose office was in Commercial Road, published the Bournemouth *Visitors's Directory* from 1858 to 1919, as well as the *Bournemouth Illustrated* from which most of these engravings are taken. BELOW: The Square in 1875. (DCL)

ABOVE: Cliff Cottage on the West Cliff, about 1863, the year after Charles Darwin had stayed there. It was built soon after Tregonwell's mansion, and demolished in 1876. (DCL) BELOW: A conversation piece of 1875, with Hankinson's new office below Richmond Hill. (DCL)

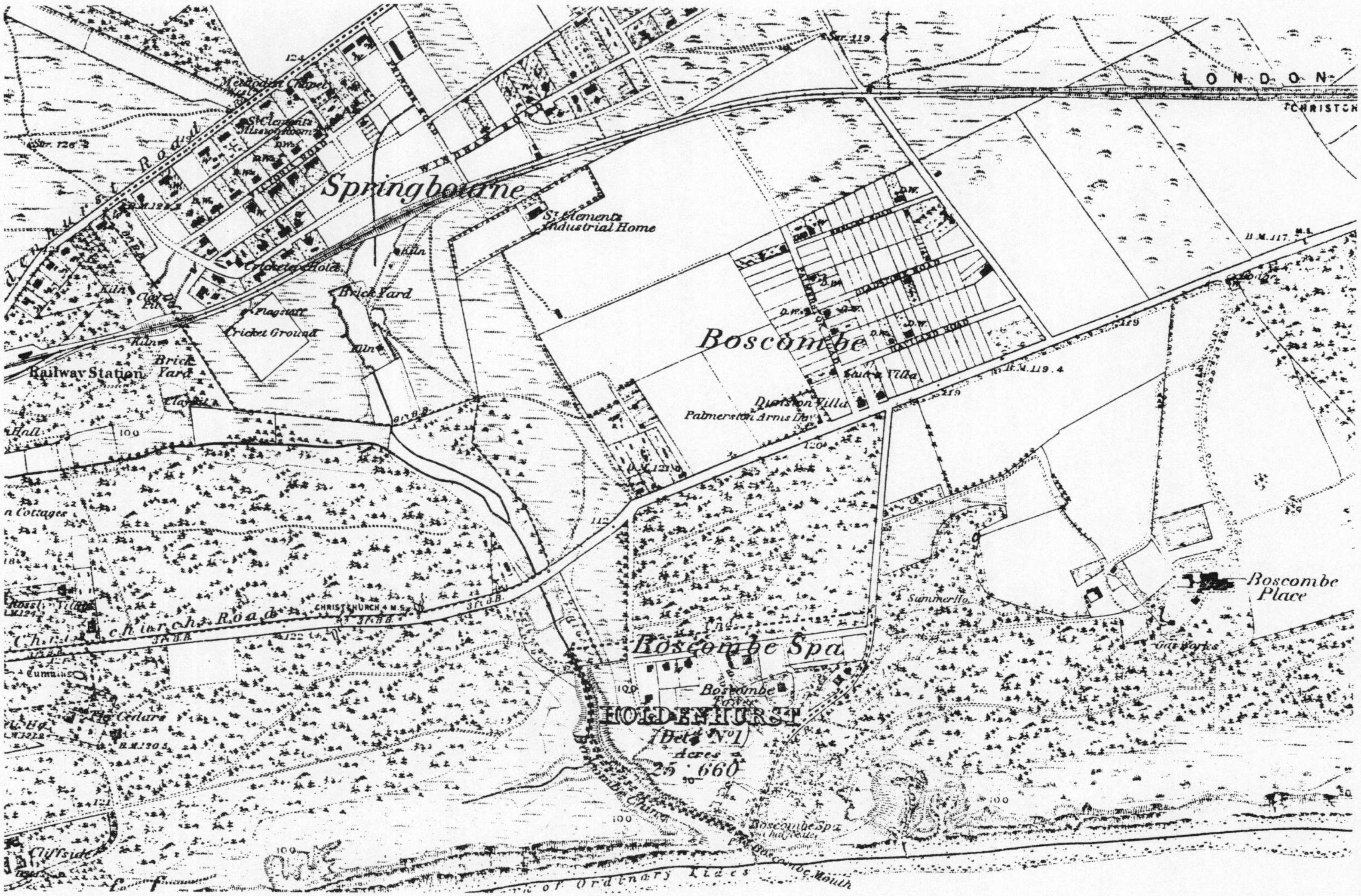

Springbourne and Boscombe, 1872: OS 6″ to one mile. Mansions stand behind the cliffs, while new housing grows at Palmerston Road; the railway to the East station divides Boscombe Heath. (DCL)

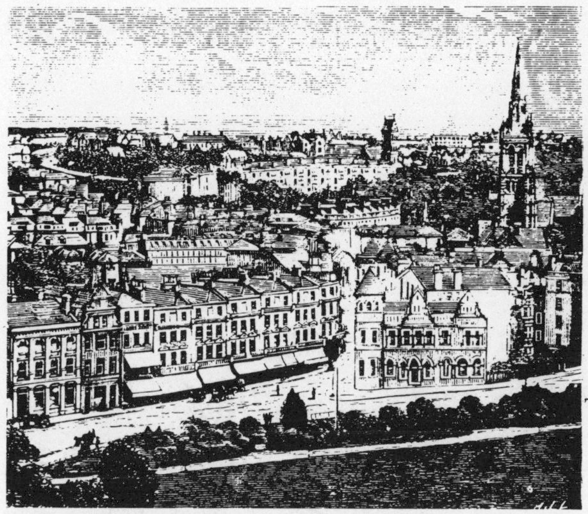

E. M. & A. SYDENHAM,

Royal Marine Library, Subscription Reading Rooms,

BOOKSELLERS AND STATIONERS,

The Pier Approach, BOURNEMOUTH.

Publishers of the Illustrated Guide to Bournemouth, 1s. : the Visitors' Guide to Bournemouth, 6d. : Large Scale Plan of Bournemouth, with References, Index to Houses, Terraces, &c. &c.

PIANOFORTE REPOSITORY.

LEFT: 1893. Southbourne Terrace stands opposite Rebbeck's office. Left of St Peter's spire is the tower of Holy Trinity. (DCL) RIGHT: 1886. The Baths were in the same building as the library, but facing south. (DCL) BELOW: The Square in 1886 was a broad street west of the Bridge. Hankinson was a Commissioner and in 1890 first Mayor. The distant Mont Dore 'bathing establishment' had been open a year when this view was published. (DCL)

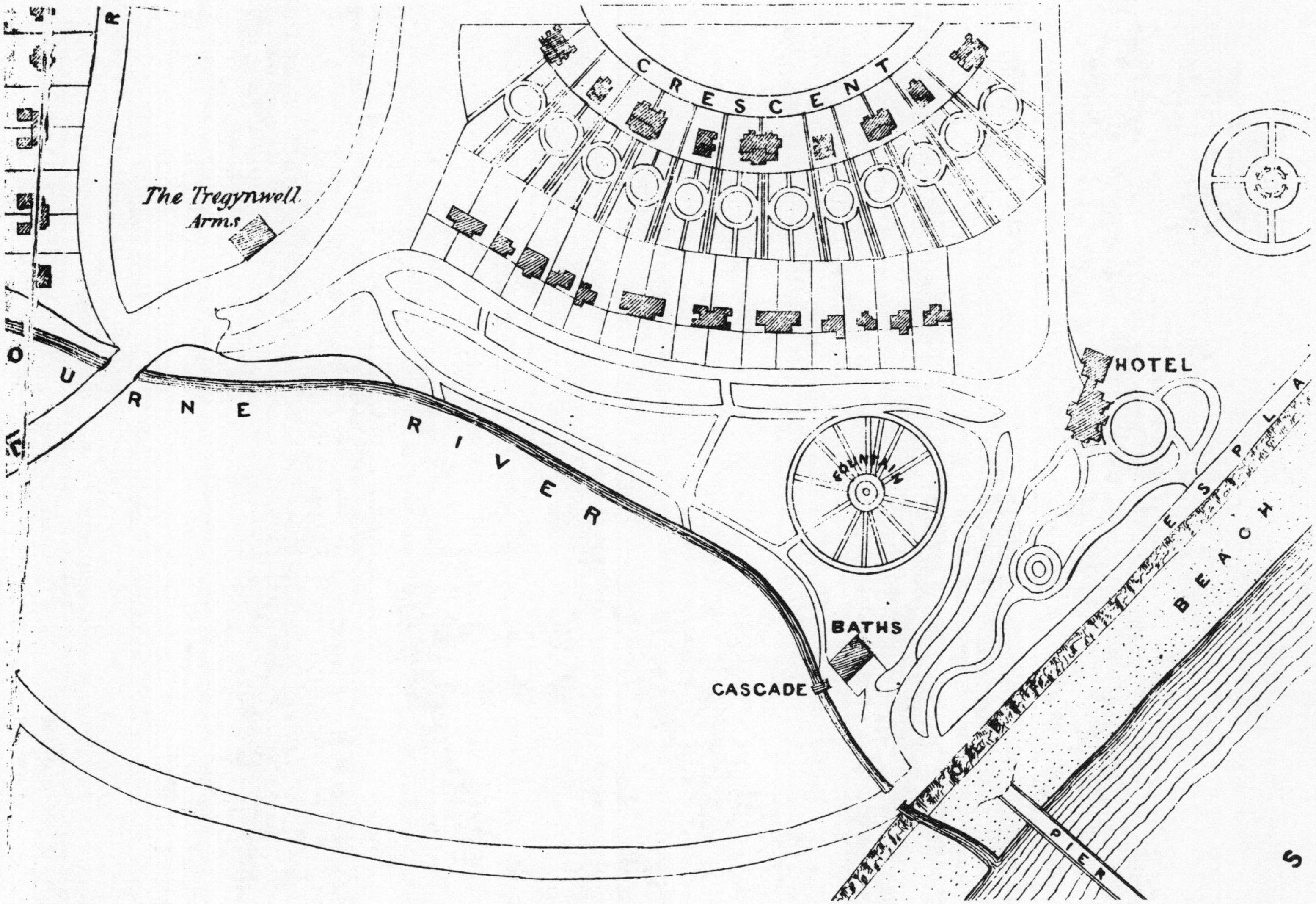

'New Marine Village of Bourne', March 1838 — Benjamin Ferrey's plan for Sir George Tapps-Gervis. The sixteen Westover Villas were finished that year, but the Crescent and Fountain were not built. (DCL)

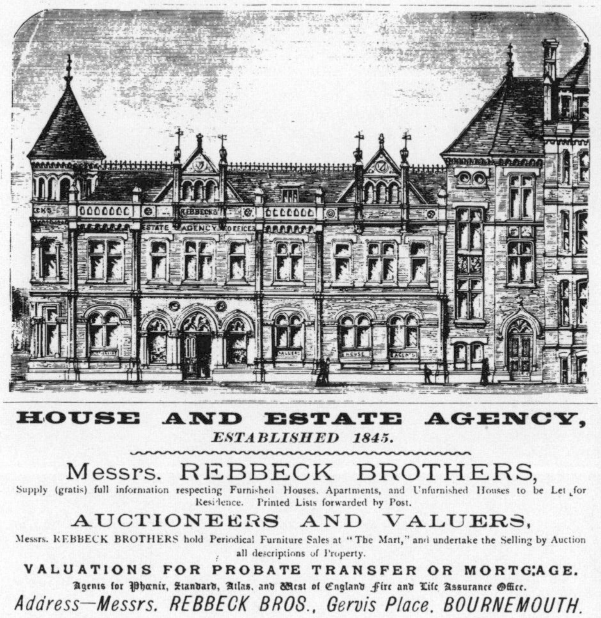

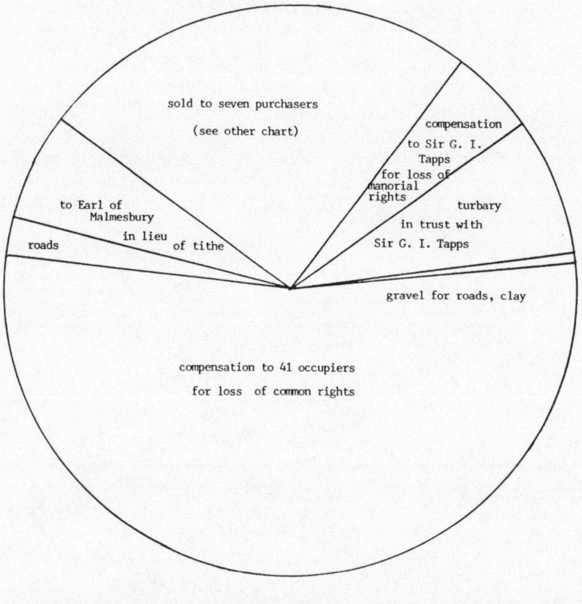

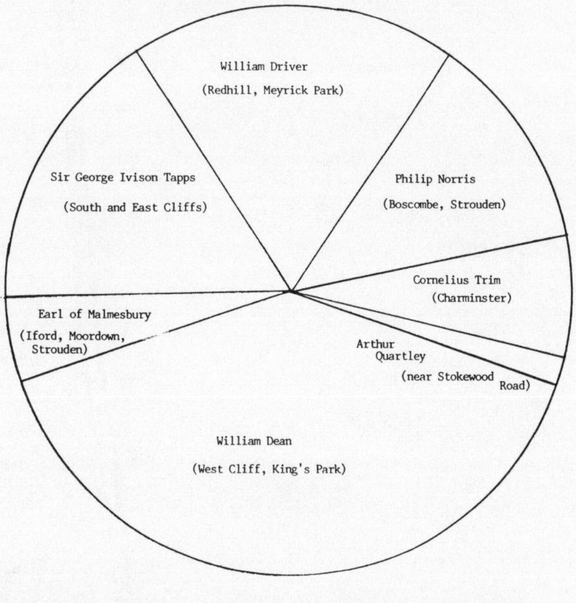

LEFT: Rebbeck came to Bournemouth from Cranborne soon after Tregonwell, as his agent. At the junction of Old Christchurch Road and Gervis Place, Rebbeck's Corner was a landmark in the Square; 1886. RIGHT (ABOVE): Richmond Terrace in 1871 had some of the oldest villas in the town, one of them Stewart's (later Norfolk) Hotel. BELOW: Hankinson's engraving shows his circulating library west of the Bridge (now the Square), before 1875. (All DCL) BELOW LEFT: Christchurch Enclosure Award 1805: allocation of 5084 acres in the liberty of Westover. RIGHT: Liberty of Westover: proportions of the 1258 acres sold in Allotments 31-57 with names of approximate areas.

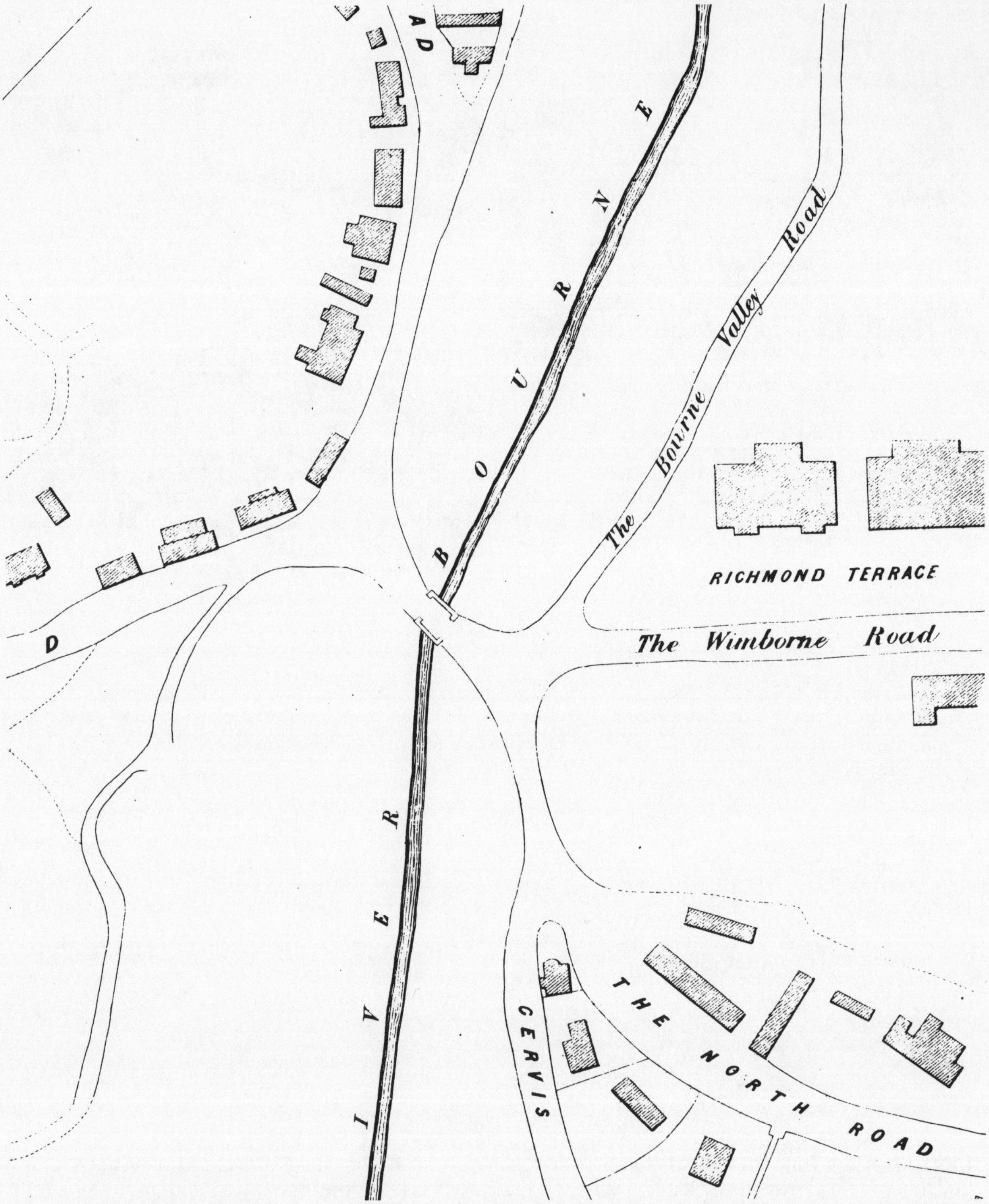

Bournemouth 1852. This extract from a sale plan shows old road names. From the bridge to the pier was 'The Tregonwell Road' (now Exeter Road). Top centre at the corner of what are now Commercial and Avenue Roads, stood the London and Commercial Inn, opened two years before. The sale involved three villas in Westover Road and two on 'The Poole Road'. (DCL)

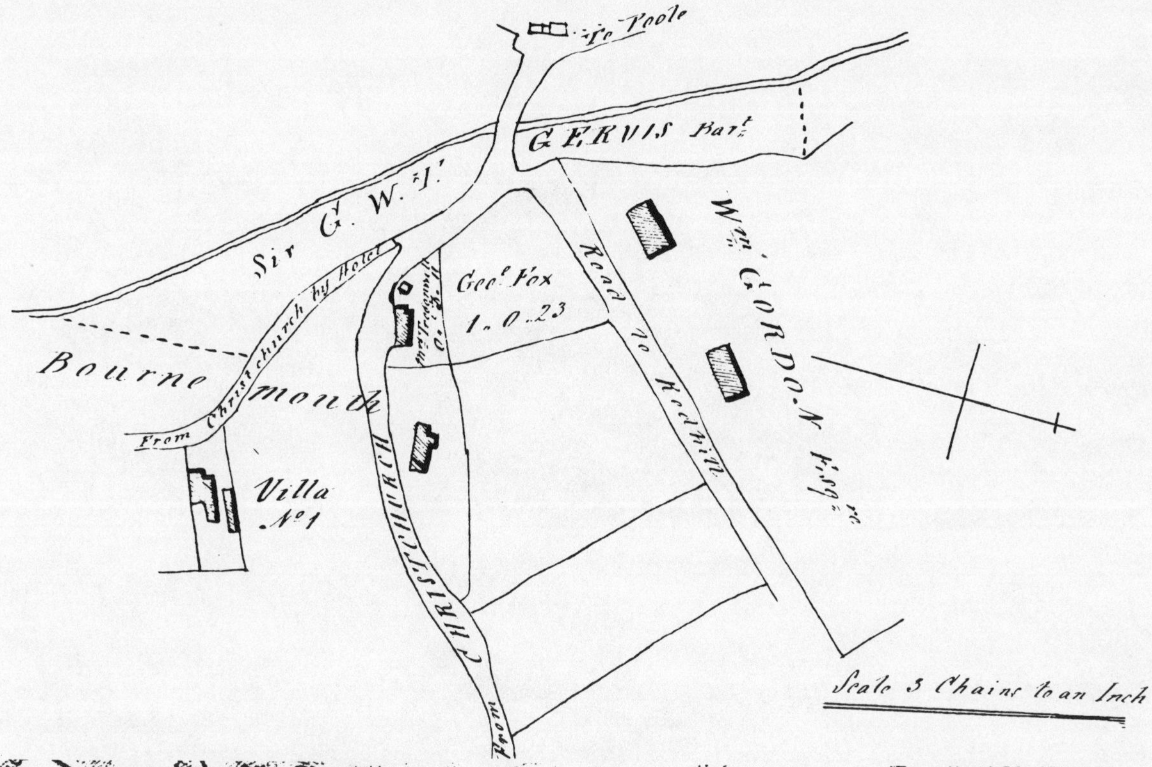

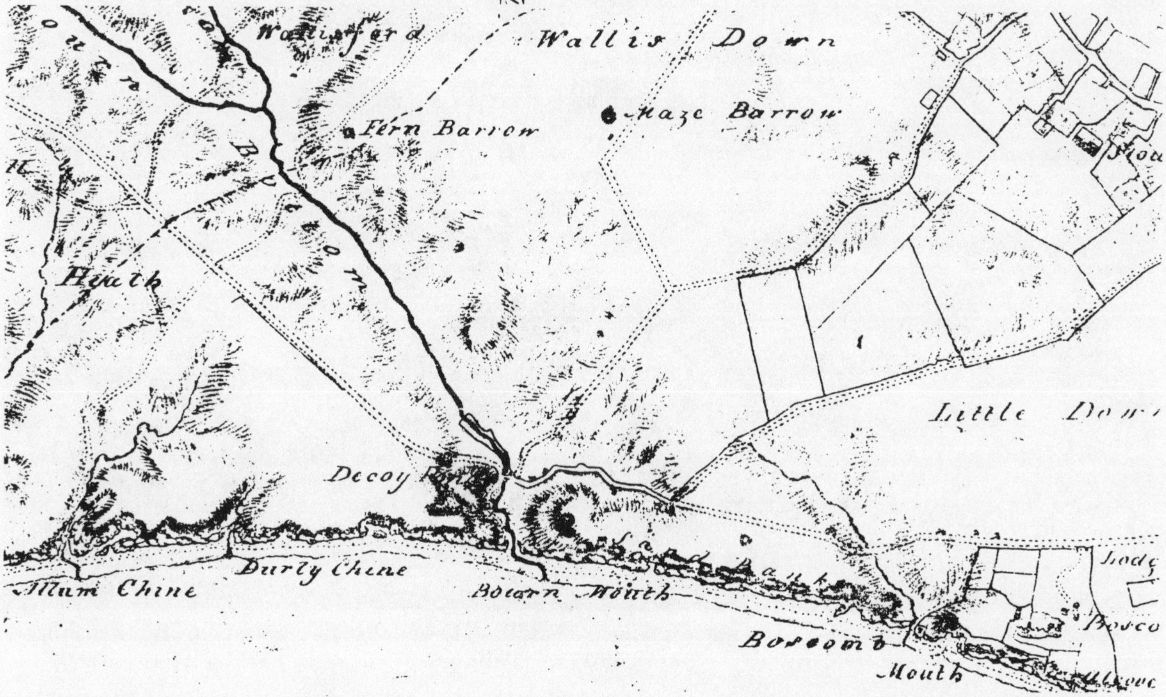

ABOVE: Town Centre, 1830s. This plan shows the inn as Mrs Tregonwell's, but George Fox bought it in 1837. Villa No 1 in Westover Road was begun in 1836. (DCL) BELOW: Bourn Mouth 1805-07; OS manuscript drawing, 2" to one mile. Enclosure Award roads of 1805 appear. Wallis Down was Poole Heath on Isaac Taylor's 1755 map. (DCL)

ABOVE: In 1865 the Bridge was the centre of Bournemouth. The space in front of the town's first shops was called the Square by 1880, though not until 1899 was half an acre taken from the Pleasure Gardens (right) to form the wide space familiar today. CENTRE: Looking west in 1865 from the corner of Old Christchurch Road and Gervis Place. On the right is the first 'Scotch' church, on Richmond Hill corner. BELOW: Horseshoe Common of twelve acres was leased from the Dean estate in 1896, and partly laid out as a shrubbery garden in 1899. The iron railings probably divided off another two acres bought by the Council for a town hall. Houses beyond are in Dean Park Road. (All DCL)

Scent of Pines and Prosperity

The first guide book to Bournemouth, John Sydenham's in 1840, referred only indirectly to its curative properties. 'The whole is softened by an air of tranquil repose and a quietude of character eminently grateful to those who seek a relaxation from the fatigue and excitement of fashionable life, or a respite from the turmoils and anxieties of rough intercourse with the world.' L.D.G. Tregonwell's work had consisted of 'an inn . . . and a few cottages, which are occasionally resorted to in the bathing season by invalids . . .'. Sydenham praised Ferrey's plan for villas, walks and drives for their comfort and elegance.

Only a year later the influential Dr Granville, who had omitted Bournemouth from his first edition of *The Spas of England* was induced to visit the place. 'I look upon Bournemouth, and its yet unformed colony, as a perfect discovery among the sea-nooks one longs to have for a real invalid . . .'. His two-day February visit ended with a public dinner at the 'Great Hotel', in which he emphasised its medical qualities; his detailed recommendations for development were respected for years to come.

'Across the valley rises that loftier range of sandhills, once barren and naked, and now covered with luxuriant and dense forests of fir-trees . . . Here must be erected commodious and well-arranged dwellings for invalids of that class who happen to be wealthy . . . Is this not the very haven that is required in England for those who tremble on the verge of consumption, or are already plunged into that destructive malady?'

Dr Granville's remarks were taken seriously. Next year (1842) the *Salisbury and Winchester Journal* announced that a surgeon had taken up residence at Bournemouth. In 1855, on a site overlooking meadows above the Bridge, was opened the Royal National Sanitorium — the second hospital in Europe to be designed for chest treatment. At first it had forty beds for female patients only, but by 1859 the *Post Office Directory* described it as 'a splendid stone building for the reception of consumptive patients of both sexes'. Three years later it was closed during July and August — 'the heat in Bournemouth would be almost intolerable'. The annual report for 1933 shows that some 240 patients were then treated, from all over Britain.

'The Sanitary Recommendations are . . . the greatest point of interest and value to the visitor', remarked Brannon's *Guide* in 1855. For residents, Bournemouth Public Dispensary was opened in 1859 at the aptly-named Granville Cottages in Old Christchurch Road, and moved ten years later to a five-bed Cottage Hospital in Madeira Vale, now Stafford Road. An honorary medical officer attended four times weekly; funds were from donations encouraged (from 1863) by an annual sermon from local clergy. No patient earning over £1 a week was admitted to benefits, though that rule excluded few when the average agricultural worker earned nine shillings. This was the origin of the present Royal Victoria Hospital in Shelley Road where, in 1874, sixty residents petitioned that it would be 'prejudicial to the interests of the inhabitants'. However, the Boscombe Provident Infirmary was opened there in January 1876 at a cost of £1,310, with a dispensary in Gervis Terrace in the main road at

Boscombe opposite the Palmerston Hotel. An annexe in Lowther Road was built in 1908 for £5,673, and after use as Avonbourne Secondary School, has now become a teachers' centre.

A private house known as the Firs, in the glen behind St Peter's church, was dedicated in 1874 as the Firs Home for Consumptives, and five years later the Hahnemann Home opened on the western edge of the town; it still exists on an island site as part of the East Dorset Health Authority.

'Instructions to Candidates for admission to the Sanatorium' quoted by Hankinson's *Guide* in 1876 show that inmates (who then averaged fifty-four) had to be nominated by a Governor, though ministers of religion could recommend one for every five guineas collected in church. Patients paid 7s 6d weekly, excluding washing. For the Hospital for Hip Diseases in Children, subscribers of one guinea annually or donors of £10 could recommend cases. The Herbert Convalescent Home, in memory of Florence Nightingale's friend, opened in 1867 and required a subscriber to give £30 a year. At the Home for Invalid Ladies, founded in 1871 at St Mary's, Dean Park, a weekly guinea was needed for each. The town's air was recommended in 1859 to 'young subjects of a strumous habit, predisposed to . . . phthisis'. Pine trees were believed to be the cure, and by 1890 there were estimated to be three million in Bournemouth.

Brannon's *Guide*, quoting from 'a popular London periodical' of 1877, assured its readers that Bournemouth's reputation for illness and invalids was fading already. 'The pleasant aspect, so I was told, would be found to be too constantly relieved with respirators and bath-chairs, pale men in shawls, and interesting young ladies, looking out to sea with large and melancholy eyes . . . but I have not seen so much as a respirator or a comforter. Bournemouth is the very place of all others where the dampest creature can get a thorough warming . . .'.

The difficulty was to maintain a reputation for ample medicine without excessive illness; disease must be disguised. The town's Medical Officer of Health remarked in 1906: 'the ambulances are as much like private carriages as is possible, and you can pass one in the street without distinguishing it'. Fire brigade horses drew the town's two ambulances. The town's Chief Sanitary Inspector blamed five cases of typhoid in 1905 on Poole oysters. The year after his self-congratulatory report, the influenza pandemic visited Bournemouth. Schools closed for a month of the autumn term, and the 112 fatalities were reckoned few for a large town.

The typhoid epidemic of 1936 was traced to an un-named dairy outside the Borough, where equipment was washed in stream water contaminated from a house drain. In July and August 284 patients were treated. Haddon Hill was prepared in three days with eighty beds, some of them in temporary buildings in the grounds. In modern, healthy Bournemouth there were thirty-one deaths.

The gardens that flow like a broad green stream from Square to shore were once an expanse of rough-grassed and waterlogged land often used for grazing. Meyrick estate papers report in August 1849 'about ten acres of ground covered with fir trees . . . and also the rough sandy ground . . . have been laid as Pleasure Grounds, the surface has been cleared of brambles, grass glades formed, and evergreen and other shrubs planted at a total cost of £527.16.0'. Two rustic bridges were built over the stream, and the area fenced in the same style, with five oak gates at which a small admission charge was made. At the same time the wooden bridge carrying the Poole-Christchurch road was rebuilt in brick, half the £100 cost being borne by the Gervis Estate. 'The Bridge' became the centre of a rising town.

A track through the Westover Plantation in 1858 soon became known as Invalids' Walk, renamed Pine Walk in 1916. Agreement between the Commissioners and the Gervis Estate led to four years' development of the Pleasure Grounds, so that, by 1873, the drives and footpaths took their present form as Lower Pleasure Gardens; a similar lease to the Commissioners acquired the meadows above, part of the Branksome Estate bought in 1851 by George Durrant, as Upper Pleasure Gardens. They stretch upstream for almost a mile, narrowing and even less formal.

Today we take the pines and shrubs as an adaption of a naturally wooded valley. Most however are due to planting schemes: the Commissioners' accounts show that in the winter of 1883-84 their Pleasure Grounds Committee spent £4 on 1,000 fir trees, £60 on 2,000 rhododendrons, £21 on turf and bulbs, and £40 on 540 feet of seating from which to admire them. A report to the Council in 1907 estimated 61,000 pines planted in the last nine years. Damming the Bourne to form an artificial lake for boating and skating was proposed in December 1881. The town was rural still: the previous month in a forty-minute run, a deer was killed a mile away in Branksome Wood.

A visitor discovering Queens Park or Meyrick Park could still today imagine he had left the town and was wandering in the countryside, since in the middle of either he could be out of sight of buildings or traffic. Meyrick Park begins ten minutes' walk from the Square, roaming over 154 acres of turf, heather and pines. In extent it has lost little since its 18-hole golf course was opened by Mrs G. Meyrick in 1894. Queens Park has been more severely pared from its original 173 acres for the building of Wessex Way.

Both these large parks, with three smaller ones, formed the five areas of turfland reserved in trust by Sir George Meyrick at the 1805 Enclosure. They were compensation for common rights lost by cottagers, and were for turbary — the right to cut turf for fuel. By 1889 only fifty-eight tenants still enjoyed the right, and coal brought in by the recently completed railways had made it obsolete. (Turbary Common at Wallisdown was not in Bournemouth then).

The 126½ acres close to the Dorset boundary had been given to the Commissioners in 1883 and, by the Bournemouth Park Lands Act which became law in 1890, the remaining eleven tenants having turbary rights there were compensated with £500. A small area was sold to raise the £13,000 needed to lay out Meyrick Park, sixty acres being made a golf course. Mate's 1898 *Guide* shows the charge was 6d for the 18 holes, annual tickets costing £1. Another seventy-six acres given by the Talbot Estate was opened by the Earl of Leven and Melville in 1921.

A Borough Surveyor's report in 1893 proposed 'opening up the Meyrick Park to the centre of the Town' by widening Sanatorium Road (now Bourne Avenue) to the Mont Dore, and making a new road from there to the park. The scheme was not completed till 1921, when Braidley Road was extended to the gardens, by taking it under a new bridge in St Stephen's Road.

At 1900 the local Corporation Act ended remaining turbary rights; the freehold of 147½ acres beyond East Common was sold by Sir George Meyrick for £25 an acre, and sixty-four acres of level ground extending towards Pokesdown for £65 an acre. The Council named them respectively Queen's and King's Park. At the former, golf links were opened in 1905; King's Park was given a cricket ground in 1902 and its main drive a year later. Both were later extended, Queen's Park to 173 acres and the other to half that size. The difference in their original purchase price is reflected in their present character — King's Park with level playing areas and sports centre, while Queen's Park remains undulating, sandy and partly wooded among its golf links.

The two smaller turbaries were of 3¾ acres, becoming Seafield Pleasure Gardens at Southbourne, where its watertower is one of the town's landmarks; and 45¾ acres of level ground sloping to the Redhill valley which was the Borough boundary with Dorset until 1931. Perhaps the most unexpected of the town's parks is the Horseshoe Common — named from its shape — which seems to have been forgotten when the business premises extended up Old Christchurch Road a century ago, and Dean Park filled with large houses in wooded gardens. The Council leased twelve acres from the Dean estate for 99 years from 1896, buying another two acres on the main road for intended municipal offices. The Horseshoe Common's wild character survived until the 1970s, when the town centre by-pass cut through it; it remains a piece of countryside, an enclave in the town centre.

The level valley floor of Meyrick Park has seen many parades, rallies and circuses. In September 1903 it was the site of a 'Grand Evening Fete' with, at 9pm, 'Magnificent Illumination of the Park by James Pain and Sons, London, with many thousands of Prismatic Lamps and Japanese Lanterns . . . Emerald and Opal Groves . . . The Park a blaze of Prismatic Colour'. Fifteen years later, in August 1918, a Military Gymkhana Fête and Athletic Sports was held there.

'Till today here in Bournemouth, carnivals have never before tried in England', announced a *Daily News* leader in July 1910. The figure of 'Chantecleer', which had won first prize at Nice, took part in the procession on the fourth day, joined by the mayors of such assorted places as London, Boulogne and Salford. Postmen's and Territorial bands led through the town. Meyrick Park had 5,000 seats, and 25,000 paid to enter. The 'eruption of festivity' lasted ten days, as part of the town's Centenary celebrations, and on the last evening 'the young folks gave way to Mafficking'.

Wooded slopes rising west of Tregonwell's mansion were named Cranborne Gardens after his Dorset home. From 1862 the site was the Archery Grounds, named after a competition held there, and in 1867 it was the scene of a St Peter's school treat.

The Bournemouth Winter Garden Company planned in 1875 to build a structure like the Crystal Palace, suitable for exhibitions and stalls. Meanwhile a roller-skating rink opened there, 'lit by torches . . . an animated scene'. A year later the Winter Gardens itself was inaugurated, on 16 January 1877. The west end was a picture gallery with seating for a concert room, but the building closed within a year. Another attempt was made in 1884 with circus performances, but these did not cover maintenance and repay the building's £12,000 cost. It was advertised as the Bournemouth Rendezvous before the town acquired the lease in 1893 and bought the Winter Gardens in 1908. 'I should not like to guarantee its stability in case of a panic', reported the Borough Surveyor in 1896; 'the structure might last many years'. It was almost sixty years old when replaced by the present building in 1937.

'A baker attends four days a week' announced an advertisement in the *Salisbury and Winchester Journal* in 1826. By 1840 Sydenham's *Guide* assured readers that Bournemouth 'is well supplied with provisions and necessaries of all kinds, several shops having already been opened; and the place being within an easy reach of the plentifully supplied and cheap markets of Poole, no difficulty is experienced'. John Tregonwell in 1849 allowed a cottage to be used as a confectioner's shop by Joseph Longman, pastrycook of Hamworthy, on an eighty-year lease.

There was conflict between the convenience and the unseemly commercialism of having shops in Bournemouth. Brannon's *Guide* assured visitors in 1855 that 'with the exception of Richmond Terrace . . . and of the part lying to the south of Poole Hill, all ranges of shops or anything of a commercial character . . . has been excluded . . . The shops are at present few in number . . . current prices here will be found the same as at Poole. We hope that no objections on the grounds of exhorbitant charges may ever be made against Bournemouth'. Only four years later, the first county directories to include Bournemouth list over thirty shopkeepers, including such fashionable trades as milliner, tailor, silk mercer and several wine and spirit merchants.

In this leisured town any business activity had to be convenient but discreet. Sydenham's 1840 *Guide* had advertisements from six traders in Poole and Christchurch, but only one in Bournemouth — his own 'Promenade Library and Reading Room . . . New and fashionable music. Soda water, lemonade, ginger beer, Tea and Coffee, will be constantly supplied with the most popular and approved Novel, Historical and Biographical Works, Travels, &c. Tooth, nail, hair brushes. Bathing Caps'.

As an estate agent, Hankinson was concerned for the town's business aspect; his first *Guide* in 1876 described the new Arcade as 'frequented with visitors, purchasers and others enjoying the many novelities displayed to their gaze and the pleasures of a morning's shopping'. By contrast, Bright's *Guide* in 1902 seemed already out of date — 'The shop part of the town, even, is nowhere continuous for any distance; there is certainly a little bit of street . . .'. Kelly's 1867 *Post Office Directory* for Hampshire was anxious to promote business — 'Our steps come to the bridge (or centre of Bournemouth) where there are some very handsome and well-stocked shops'. Over eighty are listed.

The new Arcade built by Henry Joy in 1866, and named at first Joy's Folly, was the Gervis Arcade. The avenue of shops was glazed over in 1873. When Frederick Bright opened his shop in 1875, the Arcade had two dozen firms, from laceman to stonemason, glover to game dealer. An 1886 town guide illustrates Wright's the jeweller, still in business in 1984, while the brass fascia of Offer, cigar importer, was kept when the firm, established in 1867, recently closed.

The outstanding business enterprise in Bournemouth was that of John Elmes Beale. Born in 1849, son of a Weymouth ship's captain, he worked through apprenticeship to be a draper's assistant there. Refused a partnership, he chose Bournemouth as the most promising of local towns.

Renting 3 St Peter's Terrace, a new row of shops, he stocked it from his total capital of £400. Still working at Weymouth, he spent Sundays fitting up the shop, which in November 1881 his wife opened as the Fancy Fair — soon extended. In 1885 he was the town's first Father Christmas. Purchase of two adjoining shops made possible by 1906 a £12,000 rebuilding as a single store. John Elmes Beale was soon in public life as deacon and treasurer of Richmond Hill Congregational Church, magistrate and councillor in 1900, and Mayor 1902-05.

He was still proprietor of the Fancy Fair which, in November 1912, held an opening week for a store that now extended into Gervis Place, with a rooftop restaurant and one of the first lifts in the town. The old name changed to J. E. Beale Ltd, in which the family held the shares. By 1931 the store was a marvel of the town, with its row of eight lifts serving seven floors. It was the town's most spectacular loss by wartime bombing, moving to premises above Holy Trinity Church before a rebuilt Beales opened. Still under family name and control, Beales has retained the affection of generations of Bournemouth people.

Bright's was first of the shops that by the 1920s were huge department stores. Plummer Roddis, opened in 1891, advertised in 1913 as 'the largest retail drapers on the South Coast'. A branch of Bobby's opened in May 1915, replacing several small shops in the Square. In the '20s and '30s these four huge stores led the town's shopping; each had restaurants where orchestras played above several storeys of departments. Beales' toy floor gleamed with Meccano and hummed with Hornby trains. At Christmas an animated Santa Claus rode across the front of Bobby's. Beales had acquired Okey's in Commercial Road about 1919, and started Bealesons.

In the 1970s economics forced changes. Bobby's in 1972 became Debenhams; Brights is Dingles; Plummers was divided into shops and offices. Bealesons closed in June 1982, and even the Square branch of Woolworths, opened four months after Bobby's, bombed and rebuilt, closed down, to be occupied by Boots. As the Abercrombie Report stated, town centre traffic made it unsuited to shopping, relief roads have encouraged it in streets clear of cars, and behind the 1893 facade of the Dalkeith Hotel the town in 1983 acquired an indoor market.

In Commercial Road the former Bealesons building has been converted to a shopping mall, and nearby the Triangle is to disappear beneath another. The old 'bus station, burnt in 1976 and demolished six years later, is intended for a shopping mall originally named 'Square One' — and aptly on the spot where Bournemouth Improvement Commissioners used to meet a century ago. The Hampshire Centre, built for out-of-town shopping, has invaded the fields where Holdenhurst village lived for centuries, before the first business came to Bournemouth.

ABOVE: Sunday afternoon at four in Old Christchurch Road in 1921. Founded forty years before, the firm of J. E. Beale had extended towards Gervis Place. To the right is Williamson and Treadgold's store. BELOW: Bobby's opened in the Square in 1915, and to its left is Hugh King's, drapers, founded thirty years earlier. Far right is part of the Stour Vale Dairy, where Commercial Road began. (Both DCL)

ABOVE: The enticingly named Invalids' Walk was a well-known feature of the Lower Pleasure Gardens. In 1917, when too many war invalids were in the town's military hospitals, the Council changed it to Pine Walk. BELOW: Meyrick Park was the centre of Bournemouth's Centenary Fêtes in 1910. The figure of Chanteclere from the Nice Carnival led a procession through the town. Top centre is the sports pavilion, burnt down in the 1960s; the other buildings were temporary — one (lower left) resembling the Tregonwell Arms. (Both DCL)

ABOVE: 1920. The Bourne flows from Upper to Lower Pleasure Gardens; at lower centre it formed the original Decoy Pond. Less conspicuous than St Peter's spire is the Punshon Memorial Church on Richmond Hill. The large block far right was Bobby's. BELOW: Though the drinking trough has gone, Lansdowne Crescent has changed little since the 1860s. The post-office (right) is rebuilt as a bank. (Both DCL)

LEFT: The rustic bridge across Church Glen was replaced in 1866 by the Gervis Arcade. RIGHT: An early scene in the Westover Pleasure Grounds — Invalids' Walk in 1862, with a bath chair. CENTRE: Site of the Square, 1865, with shops in Commercial Road. BELOW: The central part of the National Sanatorium for Consumption opened in 1855. This view from the south shows the east wing of 1863, the chapel of 1865 and west wing of 1870. The 1886 caption refers to a 'cheerful site overlooking the Pleasure Gardens', where it is still used as a hospital. (All DCL)

ABOVE: Leverett and Frye took over in 1872 Matthew Cox's grocery business in Commercial Road. LEFT: Mate's *Bournemouth Illustrated*, 1893. RIGHT: Southbourne Terrace was built in 1863 between the foot of Richmond Hill and the Tregonwell Arms. The site is now occupied by W. H. Smith. (All DCL)

ABOVE LEFT: J. J. Allen's Quadrant is a name that has survived the store's closure. This view of 1893 appears to show a basement area using part of the natural valley called Church Glen. Far left is Old Christchurch Road; right is the post office established there in 1880 and moved to its present site in 1896; the building shown, opposite Beales, was demolished in 1908. (DCL) RIGHT: Mate's *Bournemouth Illustrated*, 1886. (DCL) CENTRE: The Lower Pleasure Gardens, 'engraved from a photograph supplied by Mr H. J. Atkins, Fine Art Depot, Firs Glen' and published in 1893. The bridge shown is still in use. (DCL) BELOW LEFT: This 1856 engraving shows the Royal National Sanatorium opened the year before. (DCL) RIGHT: Over Church Glen was a rustic bridge, replaced in 1866 by the Arcade. (DCL)

Pokesdown and Southbourne, 1924: OS 6″ to one mile. Pokesdown grew up near Stourfield House, whose drive became Southbourne Road. South-east stand the later mansions of Stourwood, Carbery and Stourcliff. (DCL)

ABOVE: Hugh King's was a high-class draper's at the beginning of Exeter Road, opened a few months before this 1886 print and surviving to the mid-30s. LEFT: The north front of the Gervis Arcade is in Old Christchurch Road. Bright's was founded in 1871 and became one of the town's major department stores, renamed Dingles in the 1970s. This view dates from 1886. RIGHT: The Arcade was built by Henry Joy as an avenue of shops in 1866 and glazed over in 1873. A gallery for a band was built over this south entrance. The entrances were modernised in 1939 and the 'pepperbox' domes since removed. (All DCL)

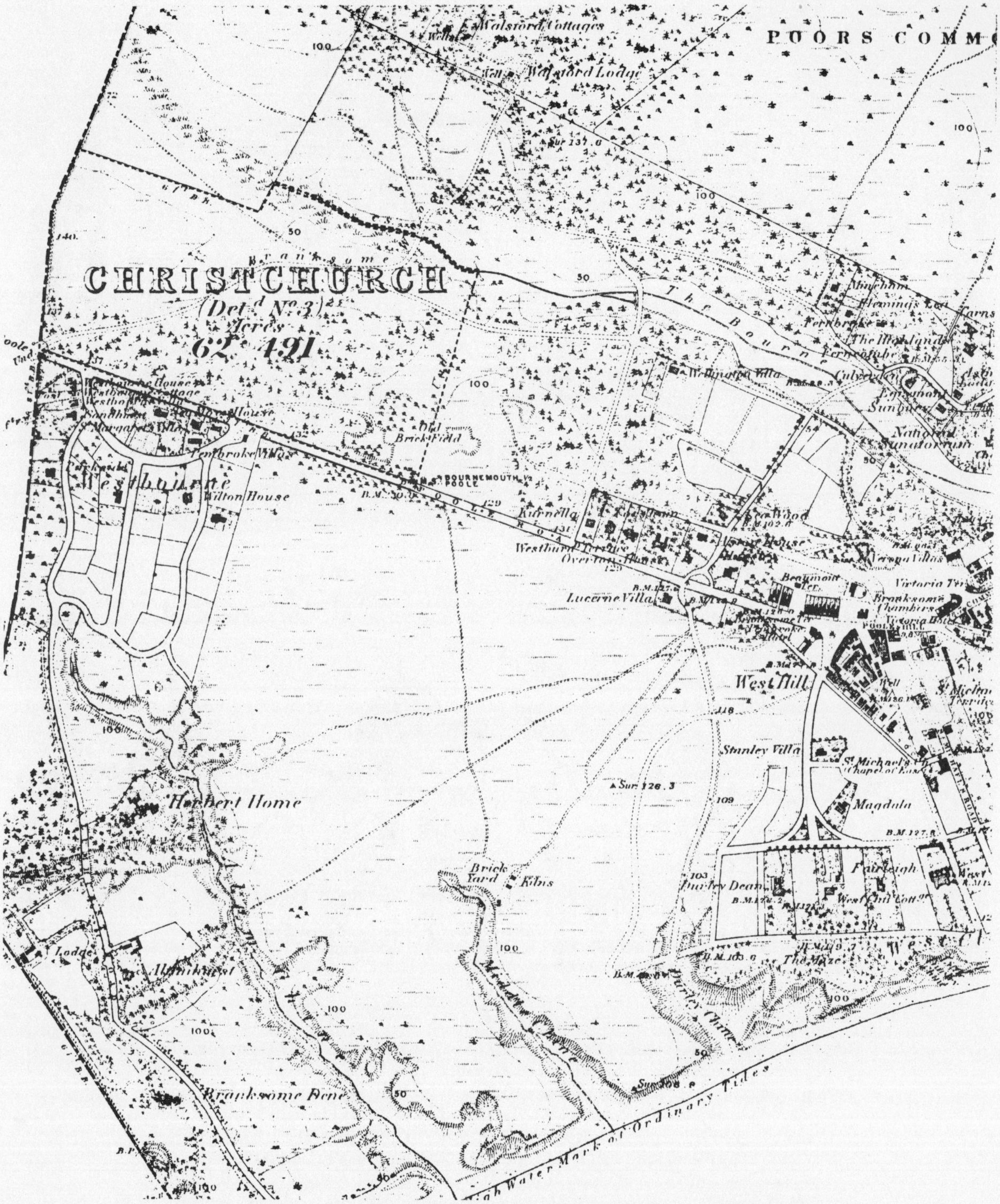

Westbourne and the Chines, 1872: OS 6″ to one mile. The Crescent at Westbourne became Seamoor Road, and Poors Common is now Meyrick Park. (DCL)

Visitors and Residents

'We have taken a house for a month called 5 Crescent. House rent moderate, we gave for one of the largest houses making up 15 beds £8.8.0 a week . . .'. So wrote Selina, Lady Heathcote in 1843 after the journey from her home at Hursley. Two years earlier Dr Granville had found 'every sort of desirable and well-furnished apartments and convenience . . . six guineas per week are charged for the season'.

In hotels the visitor had a choice of two. The Bath was a 'very elegant, spacious and convenient structure . . . a great number of inmates'. The Belle Vue Boarding House was for those 'who may prefer the retired and quiet mode of life'. Both were opened on Queen Victoria's Coronation Day in 1838.

To Dr Granville the Bath was the Great Hotel where, at a public dinner, he planned the future of Bournemouth. He approved the hotel's principal floor, but not the rooms above it with 'rattling servants running up and down, stamping with their heavy boots'. In 1856 the future King Edward VII, aged 15, at the start of a supposedly private walking tour, arrived before his rooms were ready and held the steps for Miss Toomer to put up curtains.

Twenty years later Merton Russell-Cotes stayed at the Bath Hotel, and bought it on Christmas Day 1876. He saw the building as a gallery for his art treasures, enlarging it in 1880 with 'two noble wings'. A London journalist admired 'the pillared dining room . . . replica of the Egyptian Hall at our own Mansion House'. In 1889 *The Architect* remarked that 'the artist . . . has made the ground floor reminiscent of Pompeii'. A Boston newspaper reported: 'The most elegant, most artistically decorated and furnished hotel we have seen is the Royal Bath Hotel in Bournemouth, England'. There was an embarrassing moment in 1881, when the ex-Empress Eugenie recognised a cabinet from her boudoir at St Cloud.

At the town's business end, the London and Commercial Inn was open by 1850. Soon called the London Hotel, it survived to 1928 at the junction of Poole Hill with Avenue Road. Further up the Poole road the Victoria Family and Commercial Hotel was open by 1867 and, 'at the western entrance to the town', the Pembroke by 1880. Brannon's *Guide* that year praised the Lansdowne Hotel, then some twenty years old: 'though not pretentious in character, it leaves nothing to be desired'. Meanwhile a 'monster hotel . . . under spirited management' had opened late in 1874. This was High Cliff Mansions, now the Highcliff Hotel, which has taken over a relic of old Bournemouth, the coastguard cottages.

Adapting another old building, Henry Newlyn, owner of the Kings Arms at Christchurch and lessee of the Belle Vue, opened Newlyn's Exeter Park Hotel in 1870. This was the Tregonwells' original mansion of 1812, which the Marchioness of Exeter had leased about 1820. Newlyn added a wing in 1876 and, after completion with a tower ten years later, it was palatial enough to receive the Empress of Austria and her daughter. With thirty servants and seven tons of luggage they occupied all thirty-six rooms for ten days in April 1888. The *Bournemouth Observer* noted that 'the Royal visitors honoured Mr Newlyn by placing their autographs in the visitors' book' — which is now in the County Library's care.

In 1882 the Firs, a private house, was converted to the Grand Fir Vale Hotel. With 200 rooms and extensive gardens it remained until the 1960s, when its site in Fir Vale Road was redeveloped. When the direct railway opened in 1886, a London visitor described how he telegraphed half a dozen hotels, finding the last room at the Chine. At the Mont Dore 'the lunch was admirable, and the room was filled with the bearers of well-known London faces. Curious how much at home one feels . . .'.

The Mont Dore (named after a French spa) took four years to build and cost over £60,000. The foundation stone had been laid in May 1881 by King Oscar of Sweden and Norway, here for his health, and the Mont Dore considered itself a 'Residential and Bathing Establishment' more than a hotel. With its own sea-water supply, it offered a variety of baths as well as winter gardens and covered tennis-courts. It was unusual in being neither near the seafront nor a business area, but next to the Royal National Sanatorium. During the first world war it was a military hospital, and an Indian soldier remains as a reputed Bournemouth ghost.

The Mont Dore did not reopen, but became in 1921 the Town Hall. Other hotels had a less glorious end. The Central on Richmond Hill and the Metropole at the Lansdowne were bombed in the same air-raid. The Metropole was just fifty years old, and its ivy-covered ruins gave the Lansdowne a briefly picturesque air, until Royal London House was built on the site.

The town's first *Official Guide* in 1906 called Newlyn's Hotel 'the historic house'. By contrast, the Carlton was just three years old; now it is the only privately-owned five-star hotel in Europe. The Bournemouth Hydro on the West Cliff, 'in ten acres of pine-clad pleasure grounds', had a new sun lounge and marine balcony. Sir Compton Mackenzie recalled staying there from March to June 1900, when he was seventeen and straight from school. Under Dr Johnson Smythe the door was locked at 11 pm, and no billiards allowed on Sundays.

In 1906 the Hotel Dalkeith in Old Christchurch Road offered *en pension* terms of 30s a week. Henry Laidlaw had opened livery stables there in 1873, naming the hotel in 1893 after his native town. One of the oldest hotels, Stewart's on Richmond Hill, was rebuilt about 1900, and the Duke of Norfolk, who stayed there for three months in each year, allowed it to be named after him with his arms on the parapet.

Cheap staffing allowed competitive tariffs. The Centenary Fêtes programme of 1910 advertised three guineas a week inclusive at the Hotel Central. 'Separate tables' were then a novelty, deserving 35s weekly at Meyrick Mansions. The Midland — 'High-class Temperance' — did bed and breakfast for 5s. Attractions at the Manchester in St Michael's Road were 'Electric Light and Bells. Cycle House. Photographic Dark Room'. The Trescoe in Wootton Gardens offered only 'Good Piano' for 21s a week.

Meanwhile the Belle Vue, built by Samuel Bayly on an eighty-year lease, was auctioned with his other property in 1857, having 'Pic-nic houses and Pleasure Gardens now in the occupation of Mr N. S. Newlyn'. From 1875 it belonged to the town as a prospective pavilion site, and half a century later was pulled down. It had served the town for ninety years.

Several hotels were run as medical establishments. The Bourne Hall in Poole Road, opened in 1880, described itself in its brochure as Dr Edward Philpots' private residence. He attended guests as patients, who were requested 'to refrain from arguments'. Among the sixty rooms, the best cost five guineas a week, but 'a few north rooms, which are not recommended except to those of robust health, can be offered at 2½ guineas . . . During the winter the building is lighted with the electric light'. Bournemouth's reputation as a winter resort is revealed by the hotel's reduced terms from June to September.

At the head of Boscombe Chine the Linden Hall Hydro, which closed in 1983, had been the ultimate in bathing establishments, with Russian, Aix-les-Bains, Nauheim, Electric baths and High-Frequency with Static Treatment. An advertisement of 1913 gives terms from 2½ guineas a week full board for its 120 rooms, or 9s a day, where guests could recover from exertions of croquet and bowls. But by then the town was trying to lose its reputation for invalids; the Montague Hotel advertised: 'Sanitation Perfect — No visitors suffering from chest infections received under any circumstances'.

In 1939 the *Bournemouth Guide* listed over five hundred hotels and guest houses, with bed and breakfast from 21s weekly. The Carlton, Miramar and Burlington offered hot and cold sea-water baths; the Majestic had an indoor sea-water swimming pool. Opened in 1935, the Palace Court claimed over 20,000 guests from January to October 1938.

The sepia pages of that 1939 *Guide* were a late twilight of the century since the Bath Hotel had opened on Queen Victoria's Coronation Day. War closed the beaches, blackout muffled the views, and separate tables emptied. Forty hotels were requisitioned. The Royal Bath and Burlington reopened at the end of the 1946 season. The Waverley near the Central Station was still government offices, and several, like the Anglo-Swiss, were bomb-damaged. In the first post-war *Town Guide*, the Bourne Hall was one of the few to advertise, with inclusive terms of 6½ guineas a week.

In 1982 it was being pulled down; not bombs but economics hit hotels hardest. The Gordon on Southbourne Overcliff at a spot called Mount Misery opened in 1895; sixty years later, blocks of flats replaced it. The Burlington in 1939 claimed to be 'the largest and best-appointed hotel in Bournemouth', but its age and two hundred rooms were too much. Auctioned in 1960, it was withdrawn at £17,000. Two years later it was the town's first casino gambling club; in 1965 a shopping centre plan was rejected. When bought by a local hotel owner in 1984, it had 120 serviced apartments, and is a Grade II listed building.

But in 1969 the Crest Hotel at the Lansdowne, called the Round House when opened on the old Imperial Hotel site, was a half-million pound investment. With 102 rooms it was the first new major hotel in Bournemouth since 1935.

For travellers who ventured on the road between Poole and Christchurch, the Tapps Arms was built about 1809 — the second building after the old Decoy House. Its site was where Post Office Road meets Old Christchurch Road today. The Tapps Arms appeared unnamed in a *Salisbury and Winchester Journal* of March 1818: 'A small INN, not a Brewer's, to be let immediately between Poole and Christchurch, at Bourne Mouth, near the sea . . .'.

An Ordnance Survey plan of 1870 shows that Belle Vue and Bath Hotels each had a tap-room or public bar, discreetly detached from the hotel. A refreshment room on the East Beach appeared in 1873 when Mrs Bell assured the Commissioners it was 'to be a first-class one entirely . . . It would be a great accommodation, especially to ladies, and she would look upon it as a means of keeping the beach respectable than of profit'.

Rising standards of living in the 1890s put eating-out within the experience of the lower-paid. At the foot of Richmond Hill in 1906 was 'The popular and delightful rendezvous . . . quick and dainty service . . . soups, jellies etc, invalid specialists'. This Bungalow Café (above the present National Westminstger Bank) was the Cadena. In 1928 it moved to new premises higher up Old Christchurch Road, closing in the 1970s.

Across the Square, at the corner of Exeter Road and Exeter Lane for some four years up to 1914, was the Garden Tea House, run by Williamson and Treadgold. Their high-class provision store filled the Arcade with roasting fumes of coffee, opposite Bright's Stores, serving a four-course luncheon for 1s 6d. At the other end was the Gervis Hall Restaurant, with another entrance from Gervis Place. At Beales the lift served both a restaurant with oriental decor and a roof garden with flower boxes round the sides.

More expensive were hotels. In 1908 the Royal Bath advertised luncheon at 3s and dinner at 5s, while the Burlington offered afternoon tea in the Palmery for a shilling, and an eight-course dinner served at seven for 5s 6d.

In a young town, most of the business was run by men who had learnt it elsewhere. Many came from East Dorset: speculator Samuel Bayly, who at one time owned the Belle Vue and exclusive bathing rights half a mile each side of the Bourne, started life in Blandford in 1798 and had been a Christchurch draper. William Rebbeck was born at Cranborne and had come to Bournemouth in the 1830s as the Tregonwell family's agent. In 1851 Sir George Tapps-Gervis allowed him to open an office at the bottom of Old Christchurch Road, and the firm of surveyors, auctioneers and agents is still in business. From Chalbury came Henry Joy as a journeyman carpenter, to build the Gervis Arcade, another at Westbourne, the Quadrant close to St Peter's church, and Southbourne Terrace facing the Lower Pleasure Gardens.

Publisher of the first *Bournemouth Guide*, John Sydenham, was born at Honiton and was a bookseller at Poole before establishing in 1840 his Bournemouth business, from 1877 the Royal Marine Library, which the family owned to 1925. William Mate, a later publisher of town guides, came from Bere Regis; he founded the *Poole Herald* in 1846, and in 1858 his son started Bournemouth's first newspaper, the *Visitors' Directory*. Another guide publisher was Thomas Hankinson, a Londoner who came in 1858 for his health. His business was at Victoria House in Exeter Road as a stationer, and later as an estate agent at the foot of Richmond Hill.

A. J. Abbott came from Warminster in 1865, walking from Christchurch to Bournemouth past the future site of his agent's office, opened at Boscombe in 1876. One of his earliest developments was the Stoufield estate and, as Chairman of the Christchurch Land Society and later the South Coast Land Society, he laid out much of Boscombe and Moordown. He gave Woodland Walk to the town, and could recall shooting duck over Fisherman's Walk.

The estate agents Fox and Sons from near Basingstoke, opened their first Bournemouth office at 38 Holdenhurst Road in 1889. Founder of a still-existing firm, G. E. Bridge had brought his pharmaceutical business from Chichester, and Frederick Bright, born at Bocking in Essex, had retired from missionary work in India. His Lymington business opened a branch dealing in needlework and wool in the Gervis Arcade, occupying four shops there by 1894, and expanding into one of the town's large department stores.

Perhaps Bournemouth's busiest newcomer was Merton Russell-Cotes, remembered today by the art collectgion he gave to the town. Bronchitis brought him to Bournemouth in 1876, aged thirty-one and, as son of Wolverhampton ironmaster Samuel Cotes, he quickly recognised what the town needed. He identified the Town Surveyor, Christopher Crabbe Creeke, as 'leading light . . . all in all . . . Father of Bournemouth', and engaged him to add two wings to the Bath Hotel, which Russell-Cotes had bought soon after arriving. In the visitors' book Oscar Wilde commented: 'You have built and fitted up, with the greatest beauty and elegance, a palace, and filled it with gems of art, for the use and benefit of the public at hotel prices'.

Five years after arrival, Russell-Cotes was elected to the Board of Commissioners, pressing for an Undercliff Drive scheme. Recalling a three-quarter-hour wait at Ringwood for the notoriously slow train to Bournemouth, he urged completion of a direct line from Brockenhurst. When in 1891 the first Mayor was elected — 'shrewd, long-headed Mr Hankinson' — Russell-Cotes gave the new Borough's mace and mayoral badge. Three years later Russell-Cotes was Mayor himself, third Honorary Freeman in 1908, and knighted the following year. In 1911 the *Bournemouth Guardian* described him as 'that old warrior in the van of progress'. To mark completion of the first Undercliff Drive in 1907, he and his wife gave their art collection and their home to the people of the town they had helped to make.

Though Westover Road is on the eastern side of the Bourne, it took its name from the Liberty, which from Christchurch was over the Stour to the west. (The Enclosure Award misnamed it West Stour, and the Ordnance Survey continued the error). The route named on a sale plan of the 1830s as 'road from the Hotel' became known as Westover Road.

Sydenham in 1840 was describing it when he noted a range of villas to which 'are attached ample gardens, while in the front are shrubberies tastefully laid out . . .'. These were the villas described by the *Salisbury and Winchester Journal* in July 1838 — 'The projected range of villas at Bourne Mouth are in a state of active progress'. To Brannon in 1855 'The first portion are Italian and those at the southern end Elizabethan . . .'.

In a sale at the Bath Hotel in 1852 No 6, Westover villas had '4 best, 7 secondary and Servants' Bedrooms, 2 Dressing Rooms, 2 Water Closets, Housekeepers Room, Servants Hall . . . Coach House, 3-stalled Stable and Garden' with lawn, shrubbery and carriage approach. All this had been let for £120 a year, with an eighty-year lease expiring in 1917. Villas were numbered to sixteen. The 1871 directory shows many as lodging-houses, though two were occupied by clergymen, one the 'Scotch minister'.

Westover Road remained as villas to 1905, though Henry Mooring Aldridge (there in 1871) converted Nos 1-2 to solicitors' offices which, in rebuilt form, are still on the site. In 1910 the Westover Palace and Rink opened where Nos 3-8 had been, and remaining villas had gone by the 1930s. The Palace Court Hotel in 1935 completed the transformation.

Bournemouth had always been a town of villas. In Stevens' *Directory* of 1894 some two thousand are listed, with romantic or dignified and often inexplicable names. Sydenham in 1840 described them as 'each marked by distinct and peculiar architectural features'. Granville, remarking on 'the little villa of Mr Drax', warned landowners: 'You must not let in strangers and brick-and-mortar contractors, to build up whole streets of lodging-houses, or, parades, or terraces interminable . . .'.

The terraces were built. Granville had written that 'a regular community or village must be encouraged to come and settle here, bringing along with them all the necessary and useful arts and trades'. Richmond Terrace on Nurse-hill (Richmond Hill) was there by 1855 and, ten years later, Southbourne Terrace was completed as a row of six shops with accommodation above, facing the Bourne meadows. Victoria Terrace was in Commercial Road.

Lansdowne Villas in Christchurch Road, mentioned by Brannon's *Guide* in 1863, was the first use of that important centre's name. The Lansdowne was the point where the long climb of Old Christchurch Road was joined by the road that crossed the Bourne near the Belle Vue. Tracks to Holdenhurst, and towards Redhill and Winton, also diverged from the Lansdowne. The name was borrowed from the city of Bath, in the hope that Bournemouth would be as famous for curative waters — a motive for naming the Bath Hotel itself.

About 1865, Lansdowne House was built facing south-west towards the Bournemouth roads. A crescent existed by 1870, with segments of garden in front long ago quarried for public lavatories — most of them in Bournemouth were built discreetly underground. The original Lansdowne House was occupied to 1890, and replaced by the Metropole Hotel in August 1893 — itself destroyed by bombing in May 1943. The office block Royal London House filled the site in 1957. The Imperial faced it until replaced by the Round House Hotel (now Crest Hotel) in 1969.

Holdenhurst Road (in early days called Littledown Road) approached completion after the 1860s, when the enterprising Henry Joy built semi-detached villas rented for £15 a year. Enoch White's nursery lasted until the 1890s. About 1877 Joseph Cutler built a terrace on the south side of Old Christchurch Road, naming it after himself. 'A brilliant idea . . . in having his own portrait executed in coloured tiles, with arabesque accompaniment on each pilaster in a range of shops . . . must be seen to be appreciated' was the press comment on Joseph's Terrace. His multiple portrait must be still there, hiding under new shopfronts.

LEFT: Crest Hotel, opened as the Round House in 1969, from the steps of the 1913 Lansdowne Library. Most of the illustrations in this book are from the County Library's collection. (A) RIGHT: Lansdowne Hotel was built soon after 1860 at the corner of Old Christchurch Road and Lansdowne Crescent, seen here in 1893. (DCL) CENTRE: In this 1886 view the Royal Bath had been reopened after extensions in 1880. (DCL) BELOW: Entrance front of the Royal Bath Hotel in 1984. (A) OPPOSITE ABOVE: 1934. In front of St Peter's spire is the white block (1931) of Beales; near the top of the view stands the Lansdowne clock tower, from where Christchurch Road leads eastward. (DCL) BELOW: 1925. The clock tower marks College and Library, but two hotels, Imperial (lower centre) and Metropole, have gone. Lower right are the old premises of the girls' grammar school. (DCL)

ABOVE: The Square from London Hotel before trams arrived. To form the Square half an acre had been taken from the Pleasure Gardens, the site of a decoy pond on early maps. (DCL) BELOW: The view from Richmond Gardens shows St Peter's without its spire, and the tower detached from the nave. The gable end (lower right) advertises Laidlaw's Riding Establishment, across the road from Thick's the bootmaker and the Iford Dairy. (DCL)

ABOVE: View from the tower of Holy Trinity over Lorne Park Road, where villas remain today as flats and offices. BELOW: Stewart's Hotel advertised in 1886 was renamed in 1900 after the Duke of Norfolk, who spent long periods there. (Both DCL)

LEFT: The Highcliff Hotel advertised in 1886 had been opened twelve years before as Highcliff Mansions. (DCL) RIGHT: Newlyn's Hotel, opened in 1870 in the mansion built by Lewis Tregonwell, had been extended with wings and a tower when advertised as the Royal and Imperial Exeter Hotel in 1893. (DCL) BELOW: When advertised in 1886 the Mont Dore had been open a year. In 1914-18 it was a military hospital, and the Council bought it for a Town Hall in 1921. (DCL)

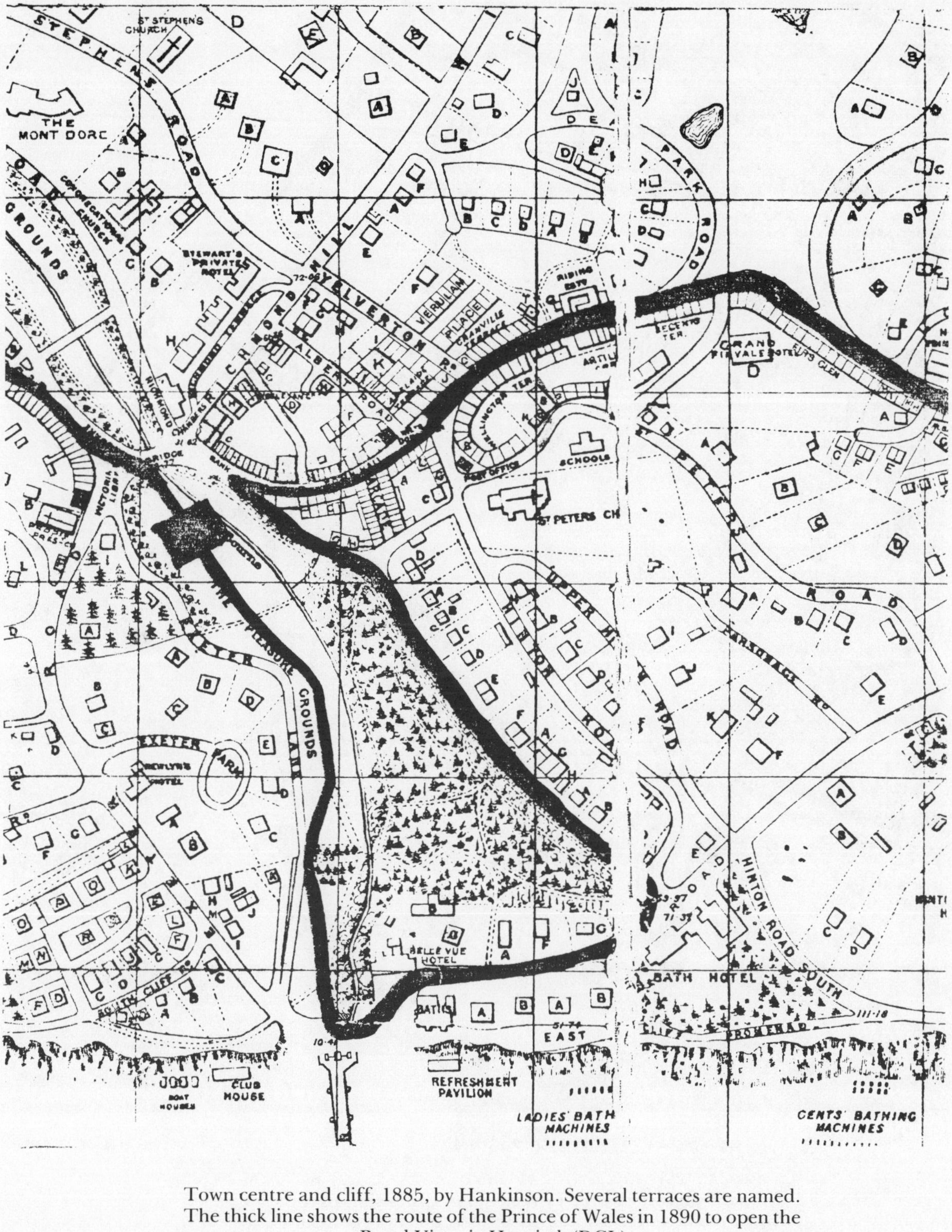

Town centre and cliff, 1885, by Hankinson. Several terraces are named. The thick line shows the route of the Prince of Wales in 1890 to open the Royal Victoria Hospital. (DCL)

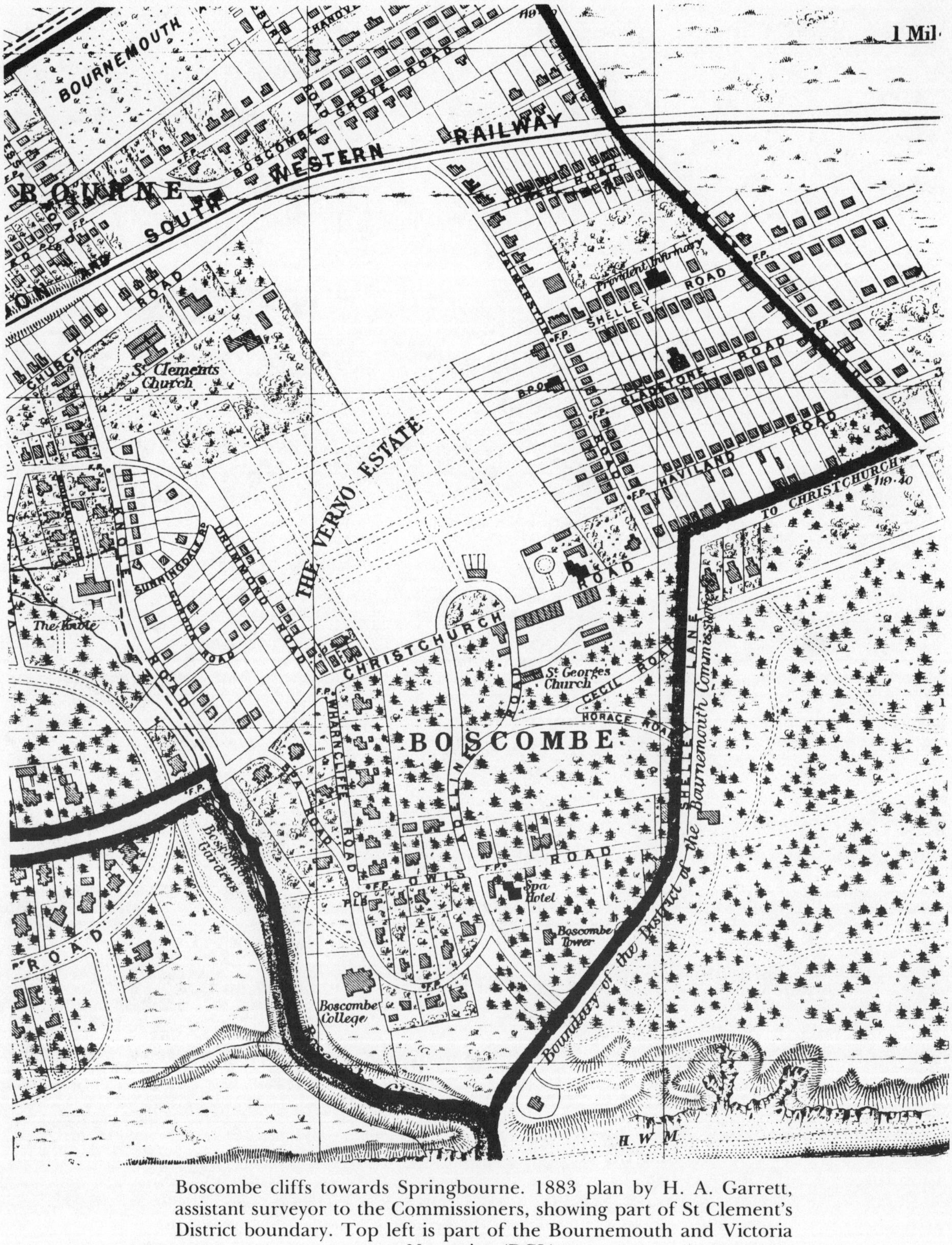

Boscombe cliffs towards Springbourne. 1883 plan by H. A. Garrett, assistant surveyor to the Commissioners, showing part of St Clement's District boundary. Top left is part of the Bournemouth and Victoria Nurseries. (DCL)

All the Amenities

By the 1850s, many of Bournemouth's oldest inhabitants had been there almost fifteen years. Already they were concerned at the number of newcomers; land sales and spreading villas did not fulfil 'the regular formation of a village' that Dr Granville prophesied. Unlike most young towns, Bournemouth had grown not from an ancient village centre, but as an outpost on a distant shore. Roads, drains and lighting needed planning.

At the Belle Vue in August 1854 a meeting agreed to ask Parliament for a Bournemouth Improvement Act. For a rate of not more than 3s in the £, a Board of Commissioners would be authorised to provide for a small town. The Act of 1856 foresaw a supply of gas (but not water), fire engines, a market and a pier or jetty. The last was the most attractive plan, since it would give communication with the outside world.

The centre of Bournemouth's own little world was to be the front door of the Belle Vue Hotel, and the Commissioners' District a semi-circle of a mile's radius from that point. The Board itself consisted of the Lord of the Manor of Westover, his nominee, and eleven named residents. Local government in Bournemouth began with their first meeting at the Belle Vue on 30 July 1856. C. C. Creeke was appointed Surveyor and Inspector of Nuisances, as well as Architect and Civil Engineer — for £50 a year, eventually raised to £300 before he resigned in 1879. Four years later he was elected a Commissioner, serving to his death in 1886. More than anyone else, Creeke was responsible for the town's layout while its population increased by some twenty times. For most of that period the Commissioners met at his house, Lainston Villa at the corner of Exeter Road.

In 1882 Joseph Cutler first suggested that Bournemouth should petition for municipal status. Boscombe and part of Springbourne were now in the Commissioners' District; it had over seventeen thousand people, who had to apply to Christchurch for poor relief, the parish doctor, County Court and police business, registration, licensing and even parliamentary votings. Petitions to the Privy Council failed in 1885 and 1887 but, when in 1888 the town might become an urban district of the county council, little opposition appeared and a Charter was granted.

On Wednesday 27 August 1890, in a saloon coach of the LSWR, the Charter was brought from London and taken in procession of tableaux, heralds and eight bands through the new Borough's main streets. At the Pier entrance the Town Clerk, James Druitt, whose family had been Clerks to the Commissioners since 1861, read the Charter. First municipal elections on 1 November 1890 were to provide eighteen councillors from six wards. When, nine days later, the Borough Council first met, Thomas Hankinson, last Chairman of the Commissioners, was elected first Mayor. Next year the College of Arms granted the Borough's armorial bearings in gold and blue.

In the next ten years Bournemouth acquired the rest of Boscombe, Westbourne and Malmesbury Park, to reach nearly sixty thousand population. The 'Memorial Praying to be constituted a County Borough' mentioned that Bournemouth in 1898 had 6,815 houses and a main road almost four miles long. The town had a 7½d rate of which Hampshire took a share.

The Memorialists prayed with success, and the town became a County Borough on 1 April 1900. It now had its own magistrates and Quarter Sessions; a new courts building opened in 1914. Fifteen standing committees were set up for the Council's business. The first Honorary Freeman was elected — Earl Roberts, for his distinguished military career. Urban Councils of Winton and Pokesdown, and Southbourne Parish Council were abolished, and a completely new Town Council elected of thirty-three members with eleven Aldermen.

With enlargements as the town grew, the County Borough Council governed until 1974 when, on 1 April, the people of Bournemouth woke up to find themselves in Dorset. They were left with a District Council which had lost major functions to the County — including the largest item on the rates, education. Bournemouth would never seem quite the same again.

The Commissioners could levy a rate, but had few expenses; the average weekly wage bill for their staff in 1869 was only £4 8s. A surviving estimate for their income and expenditure for the six months ending March 1884 shows a turnover of £9,160, with the Carriage Committee buying four new carts at £20 each and three horses at £75. By 1910 the County Borough had over 1,600 employees, and the wages bill was about a thousand pounds each working day.

The growing town required a Town Hall, for public assembly rather than administration. For the latter the Commissioners, from 1858 to 1874, met again in the private house of C. C. Creeke.

In 1868 the Commissioners rejected plans by Robert Kerley for a town hall. He was from a Wick farming family and, in 1862, had opened Cranborne Gardens (now the Winter Gardens site) as an archery ground. Seven years after Kerley's plans the Bournemouth Town Hall Co Ltd opened premises in Old Christchurch Road opposite the new Arcade; the central room was nearly forty feet high and could seat at least 700. In 1886 the Company sold it for £25,000 to a syndicate, which opened it as a covered avenue with shops on two floors. Bright's *Guide* noted: 'the Avenue is becoming a favourite place of promenade, the public being admitted freely through the day, though perambulators are very wisely disallowed. A porter is always in attendance to regulate the traffic'. This was known as Town Hall Avenue, from about 1920 as Post Office Arcade, until renamed in 1952 Criterion Arcade after the hotel at its entrance.

With the first Town Hall sold in 1886, next year another seating 1,600 opened at the converted Theatre Royal in Albert Road. From 1892 the new Borough leased premises in Yelverton Road as Council offices. Two acres of land next to the Horseshoe Common were bought in 1897 for £8,000 as a new town hall site; but in only two years the Council decided it would be kept as an open space. In 1919 they bought the Mont Dore Hotel for £33,000, using it from 1921 after expensive conversion. A new Council chamber was added in 1932. As local government swelled, offices spread into more buildings in Braidley Road, to Portman House on Richmond Hill, and even to Dorset House beyond the Lansdowne.

Over a century ago, Bournemouth had a town crier. It was an unofficial post, Frank Elgar being paid 12s weekly as lamplighter and billposter from about 1865. An ex-seaman, he wore a reefer suit with straw hat and carried a heavy bell, advertising steamer services to Swanage with 'And if you want it any cheaper, you can walk there'.

Though a Hampshire Constabulary had been formed in 1839, and the 1851 census shows a police officer at Holdenhurst, PC Smith in 1856 was the first at Bournemouth. Eight years later the Commissioners' District had a sergeant and two constables, attending Petty Sessions at Christchurch. Even when in 1869 the first police station was built in Madeira Road, Bournemouth was still part of the Ringwood Division, with officers at Iford and Moordown.

More were ordered to the town for 5 November in 1879, 'taking their uniform with them in a carpet bag or other convenient form so as to disguise their being PCs. On arriving at Bournemouth they will walk quietly to the Police Station . . . one pint of beer only to be given previous to going on duty'.

A Bournemouth Division, set up in 1892 with forty-four men under a Superintendent, applied themselves to law and order. 'Bathing on a part of the beach not set aside for the purpose' deserved a £1 fine; ten days' imprisonment was the alternative for refusing to take a dog off the pier. A hundred swine fever bills arrived for police to distribute. In 1896, communications were improved by telephones at Bournemouth and Boscombe, and bicycles.

Eventually it was the largest Borough in England without its own force. Joseph Cutler had proposed independence 65 years before the Bournemouth Constabulary was set up in 1948. In a few more years it combined with Dorset Police — a move towards the general integration of local government in 1974.

When Dr Falls' house on Richmond Hill caught fire, the Poole and Christchurch engines arrived too late. This incident provoked Joseph Cutler to call a meeting on 23 May 1870 and to offer to lead a brigade. They met for practice monthly: 'any officer on duty not being in attendance shall be fined 3d'. A second-hand engine was bought for £65, and fifty volunteers were issued with arm-bands. Next year they petitioned to 'urge the Commissioners the necessity of providing a Bell to give an Alarm in case of fire, the arrangements at present for using one of the Bells in St Peter's Tower not being Considered Satisfactory'.

In 1885 the Brigade had horse-drawn, hand-pumped machines. The West engine was kept in a shed at the Triangle, another in the East yard in St Paul's Road; from 1885 to 1927 an engine was ready at the Corporation depôt in Palmerston Road. The first motor engine came in 1913, though horses were used for ten years more. A Central Fire Station opened in Holdenhurst Road in 1902, and was extended in 1937, when the volunteer system ended. Fortunately Bournemouth was not that vulnerable; in 1874 the Brigade cost under £7. But 'One of the fiercest and most exciting fires' occurred in October 1911, when Wuytack's Restaurant in Boscombe Arcade was destroyed. The police unlocked the gates, a neighbour telephoned Captain Lane's house, and soon the town's two 'steamers' and the Boscombe manual engine saved the Arcade. A fortnight later a confectioner's at 43 Commercial Road was badly damaged. Wartime bombing of Woolworths in the Square, and Beales, caused huge fires close to where Dr Fall's house had been destroyed in spite of a bucket chain from the Bourne.

'Water was drawn from a well in the house 25 feet deep', Dr Granville assured his readers in 1841. 'Water of the brook . . . is from the gravel and sandy beds below the peat on the adjoining heath, on which not a particle of manure is ever spread.'

The Improvement Commissioners' duty was to improve but, two years after taking over, they rejected sharing any Bourne valley source with Parkstone and Poole. Lack of water was a pretext for not buying a fire engine. The Bournemouth Gas and Water Company, formed in 1863, took supplies from Bourne springs and a well. Cost to consumers varied with rateable value, down to 2d a week.

From 1885 townspeople were using water pumped from the Stour at Longham to filter beds at Alderney above West Howe, and after 1896 from a borehole at Walsford near Wimborne. In the 1950s supplies were pumped near Crichel as well as from the Avon. Rain that falls onto the natural chalk reservoirs of Salisbury Plain, Cranborne Chase and the hills of Dorset becomes Bournemouth's pure water supply.

Last century gas was for light; cooking and heating were later uses. It came late to Bournemouth, when neighbouring towns had owned works for years. On 16 September 1864 the first streets were lit by gas, made from a works out of sight at Bourne valley, with a rail branch from Branksome. The pier was lit in 1880. When the Bournemouth Gas and Water Company moved to the Poole works in 1903, seaborne coal was available, and the price progressively fell. The Company was left with its water undertaking when gas services were nationalised in 1949.

When George Fox established the first post office at the Tregonwell Arms in 1839, the post town was Poole. The aptly-named Charles Satchell, postman at Parkstone for five years, advertised that he would 'deliver and receive the Post letters at Parkstone, Bourne and the Immediate Neighbourhood, and call at the Bath Hotel and the Tregonwell Arms, Bourne, every day'.

Land from the inn to the foot of Richmond Hill was the Beckford Estate, where George Fox moved the Post Office in 1848 and, when Southbourne Terrace was built on the site in 1863, he was again postmaster. The 1851 directory mentions an office across the bridge where the Poole road began, and the postmistress in 1868 had her salary increased to £80. The new post office at the Christchurch Road corner of the Arcade managed (it was recalled) 'to meet the rapidly increasing requirements of the place from time to time', with a staff of two, but by 1872 it had an inspector and six postmen.

In 1859 James Bell, grocer of Poole Road, ran an omnibus to Christchurch and to Christchurch Road (later Holmsley) station twice a day, and a daily letter-carrier called at Poole, delivering at 7. The telegraph was open from 7 am to 8.30 pm. In 1871 Brannon's *Guide* mentioned the 'brand-new Post and Money Order Office' in Lansdowne Crescent. The *Bournemouth Observer* named the head office in 1875 as the Gervis Arcade, with branches in Commercial Road, Lansdowne Crescent, Boscombe, Pokesdown and Winton. The town then had only ten pillar and wall boxes, including two at Westbourne and Springbourne. A post office stands on the site of Boscombe pound.

In the Quadrant near St Peter's Church a new head office cost £2,500 in 1880. The present office in the renamed Beckford Road opened in 1896, behind the site of the just-demolished Tregonwell Arms. In 1910 the town had a postal staff of 404, including 203 postmen and 63 telegraph messengers.

Railways made the first electric telegraphs, but in 1860 Bournemouth had neither. In that year wires were carried from the *Herald* publishers at Poole to Mate's office at the bottom of Old Christchurch Road, running discreetly underground as they entered the town. Ten years later the Post Office took over all private telegraphs. When the present Head Post Office opened in 1896 'twenty telegraph messengers in full uniform were drawn up' under their drill instructor.

A public clock was at Wyatt the watchmaker in Southbourne Terrace where 'an electric ball in direct communication with Greenwich Observatory, falls daily (Sunday excepted) at ten o'clock in the morning'. Such activity was not for a Bournemouth Sunday, when telegraph offices opened from 7 to 10 am, instead of the fourteen hours of weekdays.

Bournemouth voices first used the telephone in a demonstration at the old St Peter's school. There in August 1884 the Poole ironmongers H. Bayley and Sons showed the new telephone instruments that were to link their Parkstone, and soon their Poole Hill premises, by posts and wires along the railway. The first public call was made on 19 March 1886 from a new exchange at 1 Adelaide Villas on the corner of Albert Road to Laidlaw's Riding Establishement two hundred yards up the street. The new exchange had three operators by day and one at night, but Sunday telephones were silent after 9 am.

By 1888 call offices existed in Boscombe, Westbourne and Poole, and there were nearly two hundred subscribers in the town. The National Telephone Company took over the local service in 1892. Each week the *Bournemouth Observer* printed details of new subscribers, and an exchange opened in Southbourne in 1905. For many years telephones were still considered a luxury if not needed for business. The two grammar schools had them in 1939, and only Civil Defence requirements installed them in other schools.

An experiment in broadcasting began in 1901, when the Mayor signed an agreement with H. Bayley and Sons for an Electrophone service. Several hotels as well as private subscribers hired sets of headphones on a table trolley, connected through Bayley's exchange to microphones at the Winter Gardens, Theatre Royal and churches including St John's at Boscombe and St Michael's. When the licence was withdrawn in 1925, Bournemouth had been a BBC station for two years.

Electricity first lit Bournemouth at Dean Park cricket ground in November 1878, when over 3,000 marvelled at a local firm's demonstration of arc lighting. A generator working in 1880 was soon closed down as a 'nuisance'. It was another eleven years before the Bournemouth and District Electric Lighting Company was formed, with 3,000 lamps and sixty consumers; by 1897 the figures were 23,000 and three hundred. In that year the firm was taken over by the Bournemouth and Poole Electricity Supply Company, which lasted until nationalisation. Like gas, power was generated at Bourne Valley outside the Borough.

Several times the Council considered buying out the Company. In 1899 they planned their own supply from steam generators to light the Lower Pleasure Gardens and Pier, as well as a scheme for lighting main roads through the town from works near the Central Station. The private company promised a supply to Pokesdown and Winton after 1901, but parts of Kinson had none until the 1950s. When in 1935 the national grid was connected and local production ceased, J. C. Bayley, aged ninety, could remember his father's demonstration of the town's first telephones half a century before.

Lower Pleasure Gardens, with the new Bournemouth International Centre. (A)

ABOVE: On a sunny morning eighty years ago, walkers stroll in the Square. The London Hotel stands at the corner of Commercial Road and Avenue Road. Tram 9 is going to Boscombe. BELOW: In 1921 a bridge carrying St Stephen's Road over Braidley Road gave direct access from the Square to Meyrick Park. (Both DCL)

ABOVE: Largest of the three Victorian arcades is in Boscombe, part of Archibald Beckett's scheme. The Grand Continental Arcade had seats for musical recitals given from the gallery. BELOW: The Bournemouth Winter Gardens Company opened this glazed Pavilion in Cranborne Gardens in 1877. Eventually the whole site became known as the Winter Gardens. (Both DCL)

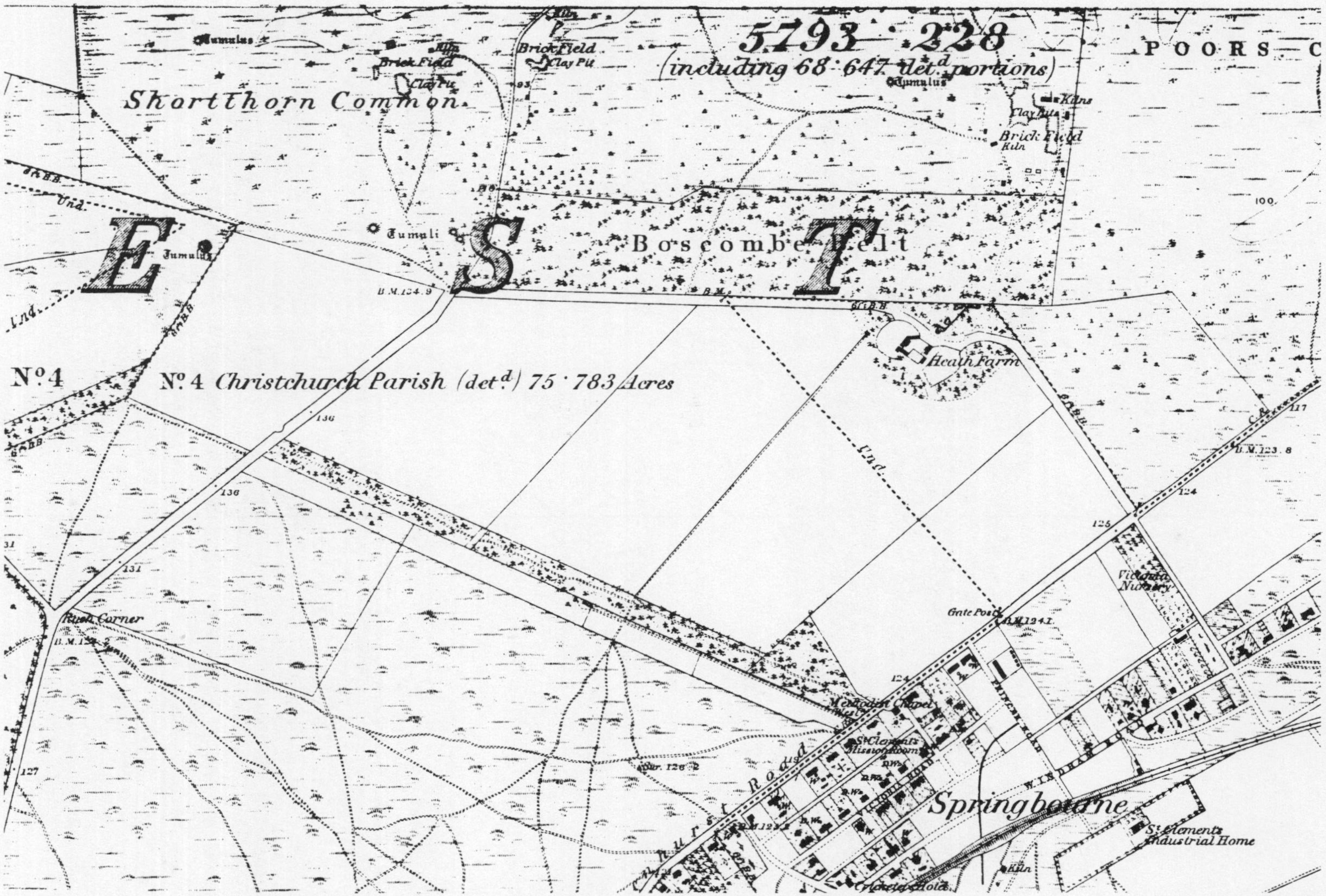

Springbourne and the Commons, 1872: OS 6″ to one mile. Beyond Holdenhurst Road lay East Common, while Poors Common was a piece of turbary land that became Queens Park. The site of Heath Farm is now Richmond Park Road. (DCL)

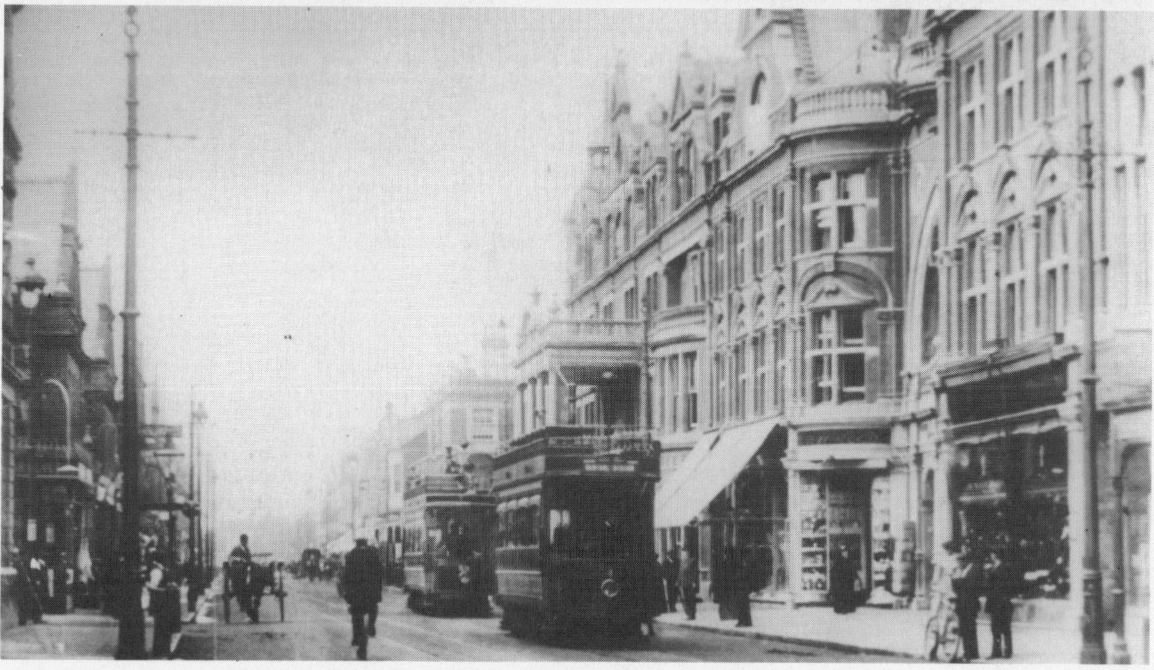

ABOVE: When the Bournemouth Municipal Orchestra was founded in 1893 the Council leased the Winter Gardens as a concert hall. The orchestra moved to the Pavilion in 1929, and the Winter Gardens was demolished in 1935. BELOW: Part of Archibald Beckett's scheme for Hippodrome, Arcade and Salisbury Hotel appear in this view of Boscombe. All were built in 1890-95 to emulate the centre of Bournemouth. (Both DCL)

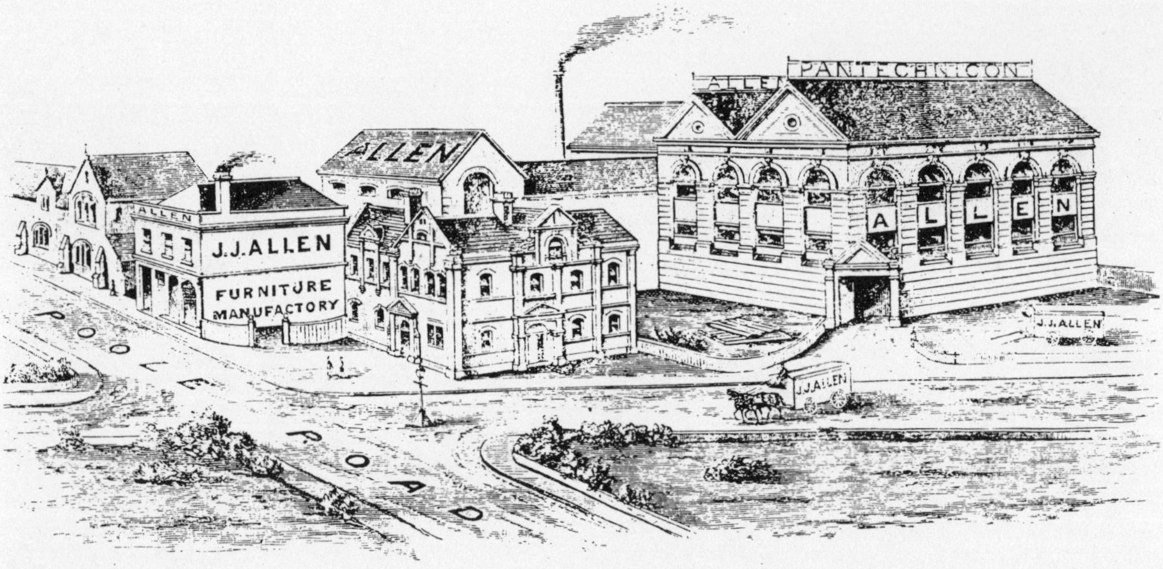

ABOVE: This was the junction of Poole Road and Crescent Road (now Seamoor Road) in 1893. The Pantechnicon is still a furniture repository (though not Allen's) and a listed building. BELOW: Boscombe Pier. (Both DCL)

Town Centre. Commissioners' plan 1883. A stream flows down the Marbarrow valley, past the Mont Dore to the Bourne. (DCL)

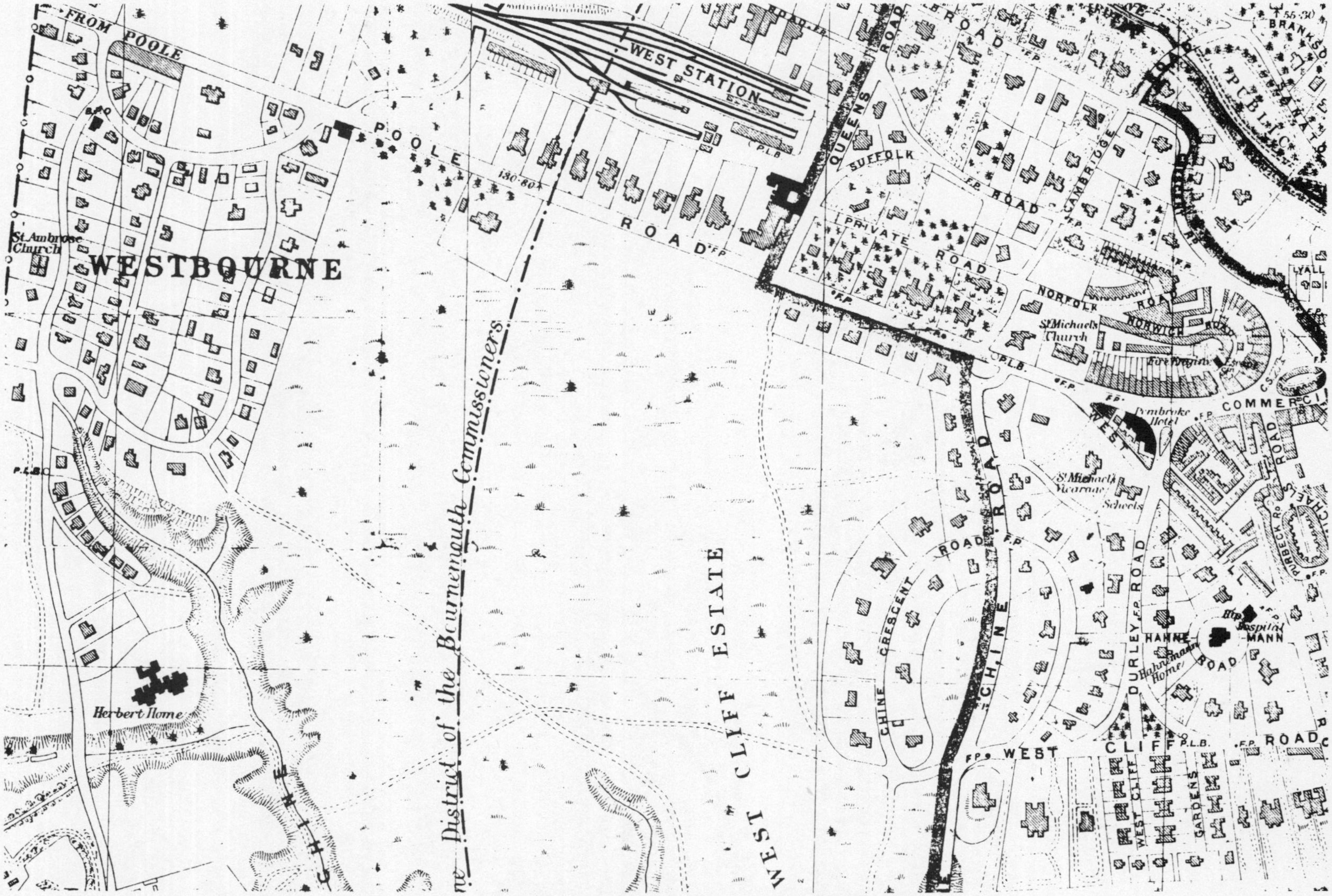

Westbourne. Commissioners' plan 1883 showing part of their District's one-mile radius. Far right at the Triangle is one of the town's two fire stations. (DCL)

Places Beyond

'It is told of a labourer of the time', reminisced a Boscombe and Southbourne brochure of 1910, 'who demanded the immoderate fee of four shillings for a day's turnip hoeing, that his master offered him an acre of land instead'.

The Earl of Southampton's survey in June 1574 of the coast where enemies might land reported: 'Wee finde more a place called Bastome wthin: the said Baye wch: is also an easy place for the ennemye to lande conteining in length a flight shott'. Next year Saxton's county map marked a Copperas House at Bascomb — copperas being iron sulphate used in dyeing and tanning. Taylor's large-scale map of 1759 names Boscomb Chine, with Boscomb Bottom the valley running inland onto Pool Heath. The Ordnance Survey manuscript draft in 1805-07 shows no building there, though by 1801 Boscombe Cottage with fourteen acres was owned by Philip Norris, who gained another 155 acres from the Enclosure Award. In 1816, on the death of a new owner, Robert Heathcote, it was advertised as 'an elegant marine villa known as Boscombe Lodge, fitted up with much taste, environed by park and upwards of 200 acres of land'.

'Boscomb Lodge, the admired seat of James Dover Esq., who, within the last few years has made extensive improvements distinguished by the indications of a cultivated taste', was Sydenham's description in 1840. Nine years later it was bought by Sir Percy Shelley, the poet's son, for his mother, the name then being Boscombe Lodge. Sir Percy, with Lady Shelley, made it their home in 1851, and helped to develop Boscombe from three cottages and an inn, the Ragged Cat, into streets of buildings fit for a town itself. Brannon's *Guide* in 1855 warned visitors that 'wild sand hills, and a naked acuminated promontory of the original cliff, form the western side of Boscombe Chine'. No part of Bournemouth has been subject to such a bombardment of developers as was Boscombe from the 1860s to the 1890s. In 1868 a mineral spring near the sea was made into Boscombe Spa, which Sir Henry Drummond Wolff had bought from the Earl of Malmesbury, building Boscombe Towers, 'a grey edifice evidently on a French model with pepperbox turrets'. Land nearby was laid out for villas, with shops for the Christchurch Road. In 1872 the first of the development companies, the Boscombe Spa Hotel Co obtained a 99-year lease; their hotel, which opened in September 1874, was greeted by the *Morning Post* as 'a new place of refuge to the tired Londoner'. It lasted only six years and, after use as the private Bournemouth College, reopened in 1885 as the Boscombe Chine Hotel.

Already development was merging round Sir Percy Shelley's property (now renamed Boscombe Manor) and the Boscombe Spa, until in 1876 the Bournemouth Commissioners took over the 503 acres, chiefly to run their drains through them. It was their first extension, and the new railway divided it effectively into Boscombe and Springbourne.

Next year, when a licence was requested for the Portman Arms in Ashley Road, it was stated that Boscombe had grown from 52 to 244 houses in five years. The water tower, (now a listed building), and the first local roller-skating rink near Caernarvon Crescent were completed in 1875, and three years later Boscombe had two public halls.

Now the developers moved in. In 1881 the Boscombe Land Society bought thirteen acres on the northern side of Boscombe Hill, naming it the Hengistbourne Estate, with Drummond Road at its centre. Sale by ballot was slow at first, owing to the bleakness of the land. The same firm in 1884 earned £18,305 from the sale of seventy plots, part of the Shelley Estate. Adjoining land was sold in 1888-90 as 163 plots, some of which cost £300 each. The Clingan Charity Trustees in 1887 disposed of their sixteen acres allotted by the Enclosure Award; the South Coast Land Society, buying it by tender, next year resold by ballot, and the site became Portman and Wolverton Roads.

Most of Boscombe had gone for development in the decade to 1890. In that year Archibald Beckett began building at its centre. The Salisbury Hotel costing £12,000 had thirty-five bedrooms, while the Grand Continental Arcade (later the Royal Arcade) was completed in 1893 for £40,000. Seats along the centre were for concerts three times daily, with a musical director and a thousand-guinea organ. Beckett founded the Boscombe Band to play there. Biggest and last of the town's Victorian arcades, it too was lined with shops. The Boscombe Grand Pavilion Theatre cost Bennett another £15,000 in 1895, and twenty years later was renamed the Boscombe Hippodrome. After refitting, it would hold two thousand.

The last of Boscombe Spa and Boscombe Manor estates were sold off in 1895. The description that year in Stevens' *Directory* of Boscombe as 'an important and rapidly rising Suburb of Bournemouth' was out of date. By 1900, when it became part of the new County Borough, scarcely a vacant plot remained in Boscombe. Eight acres in Boscombe Chine Gardens, leased by the Commissioners, had been laid out with a rustic bridge, Lady Shelley had given the cliff gardens, and Caernarvon Crescent gardens were being acquired.

In 1827, related Russell-Cotes, the Hon Charles Harris (of Hurn Court) knocked down a guillemot with a riding-whip near Boscombe. In 1910 a Boscombe and Southbourne brochure boasted: 'The long villa-dotted avenues, deep lined with stately trees, are more like Arden than Suburbia. Everywhere the hand of the vandal has been stayed . . . Boscombe has not been familiarly named "The Bright" for nothing'.

'Pokesdown' announced Bright's *Town Guide* of 1902 — 'The name is more romantic than it looks, being derived from Puck's Down, the Breezy Resort of Fairies'. Few people living in Pokesdown today would have thought of this.

At least the name is old. Churchwardens' Accounts of Christchurch record in 1663-64 that Henry Mantle of Poxdown paid them a shilling; in a 1706 baptism register entry the place-name is shortened to Pox. About 1766 Edmund Bott built Stourfield House, which in altered form still remains under the name of Douglas House Hospital, and Southbourne Road was its carriage drive. Farmer Richard Dale, born there about 1795, recalled 'that was the first mansion to be built on the common between Christchurch head and Poole'. He described its site as 'a small mound or hillock, on rising ground, on the north side of an extensive common, covered with furze, heath etc.'. The only established road was Pokesdown Lane, on the line of Stourvale Road and Clingan Road to Iford Bridge.

Between 1788 when, as Lord of the Manor, Sir George Tapps bought Stourfield House, and 1844, it was let to several tenants. In that year Admiral William Popham bought the estate, living there for the last twenty years of his life. The Popham family stayed there to 1893, and in that period of half a century the work available on the estate encouraged settlement. One of the family remembered the stuccoed house then as 'somewhat the appearance of a cardboard castle'. Farmer Dale remembered sheep on Stourfield Farm, 'feeding in Holding Bottom, about midway between Mount Misery and Boscombe Cottage, which stood in Crab Tree Close, near where Sir Percy Shelley's house now stands'. Mount Misery was a sand-dune on the site of the later Gordon Hotel.

Enough people lived near Stourfield for the Anglicans to dedicate St James' Church at the top of Pokesdown Hill in 1858, 'one of the most beautiful little village churches in the county'. A Congregational church opened the same year, though the first chapel dated from 1835, and prayer meetings had been held weekly in a thatched cottage in 1820. Pokesdown post office started in 1865, and was kept by the Bolton family for a hundred years.

In 1872 a public meeting urged a railway station at Pokesdown, where some 600 people now lived; the same year the Cromwell Hall was first used by the Mechanics Institute, which had begun four years earlier. 'The village of Pokesdown is very pretty', explained Hankinson's *Guide* in 1880, 'and residences of every description, from humble cotter's house to handsome villas have arisen'. In the ten years up to 1891, the population of Pokesdown almost trebled, encouraged by a railway station at the top of Pokesdown Hill.

Significantly, the new railway station was for eleven years called Boscombe, which had more leisured connotations and a fairer sound. Pokesdown has never been a popular name. With Southbourne (invented in 1870) and Boscombe East cramming it in, Pokesdown seems compressed to a small area near Seabourne Road, where Stourvale Road was the original Pokesdown Lane. It was linked with Winton in a surveyor's report in 1891 as having 'no system of drainage or sewage disposal other than cesspits and earth closets'. Only three roads were publicly maintained, and thirty unpaved. That year (1891) the Pokesdown Association urged joining the new Bournemouth Borough; three years later Hampshire rejected an application for Urban District status. Nobody wanted Pokesdown. But in 1895 it graduated through parish to urban district, and Pokesdown tried to be a town. The council even wanted its name changed to Pinecliff.

By 1897 Pokesdown's population was estimated at nearly 5,000, and some of its 1,100 children attended Freemantle National School, opened the previous year. Freemantle as a name is almost lost, with only a hall in Somerset Road to recall it.

Even the name of Pokesdown might have gone. When its ratepayers voted to accept Bournemouth's offer to absorb it, one warned that 'if it is incorporated within Bournemouth it would simply be blotted out and in future no-one would know that Pokesdown ever existed'. In November 1901 it became part of the Borough. The name has not been 'blotted out', though it was not popular as a residential address; the public library there is named Southbourne. The unplanned line of Seabourne Road opens with a breath of relief into the broad, curving boulevard of Southbourne Grove. The station was renamed Pokesdown in 1897, though its neighbourhood prefers to be Boscombe East.

If there was a Westbourne there should be an Eastbourne, but somewhere in Sussex had used the name. So when, in 1870, the Southbourne Land Company promoted by Dr Thomas Armetriding Compton bought 230 acres from General Cleaveland, he called it Southbourne. It had over a mile of shore stretching east from an old smugglers' track on the site of Clifton Road, reached by a cliff path.

The oldest estate was Stourfield, whose woods touched those of Carbery. Another mansion, Stourcliff, remains in Ken Road, though its twenty acres are modern housing. Stourwood, whose land lay between the cliff and Hunter's Wood (now Southbourne Grove), is now called Southbourne Manor in Stourwood Avenue. In 1872 Sir Henry Reeve, visiting his friend Lord Cairns in Manor Road, noted in his diary: 'Rode to Hengistbury Head and saw for the first time, the Southbourne Estate'. The house he built and occupied in 1876, on a site already known as Foxholes, was the last of the mansions and survived until the 1980s.

Writing in 1914 his story *Southbourne's Infancy*, Dr Compton recalled many remains of pigsties, which he thought might have been used for breeding rabbits. Local landowners had discouraged cottage-building; there were only three such dwellings and a coastguard station. More surprisingly, few lodging-houses existed.

Foxholes stood close to Belle Vue Road, which Dr Compton had constructed for access to Tuckton. The toll bridge there was completed in 1883 by the Tuckton Bridge Company. The same year the Sourthbourne Land Company began an undercliff esplanade, two years of work and £15,000 producing a third of a mile of road above a sea wall. Below the cliff the Company built a terrace of six houses, and Dr Compton showed his confidence by living in one of them from 1888-92. Known as Undercliff West, they lasted out the storms to 1897. The Southbourne Pier Company's £4,000 venture, 300 feet long, lasted intact only from 1886 to 1900; in the week the century turned, it was damaged twice by storms. The Council declined to buy its wreck in 1907, and demolished it for safety.

For years Southbourne's attraction was its own Winter Garden, a glass conservatory 400 feet long, opened in 1874 on the present site of Bolton Road. Bright's *Guide* in 1888 advertised: 'The Omnibuses for Bournemouth leave the Winter Garden at 10,1 and 4.30.' — and admission was 6d. Southbourne's Winter Garden led Bournemouth by three years.

Until the first Tuckton Bridge was completed in 1883, the bridge at Iford was the lowest crossing of the Stour. Charters of Baldwin de Redvers in 1140 and 1160 refer to the 'pontem de huver', and other spellings include Ever, Luvre, Yver and Ifford. Leland's *Itinerary* about 1540 noted 'Iver Bridge of Stone'. Holdenhurst was responsible for upkeep of one arch on the Christchurch side. When rebuilding was proposed in 1784, Hampshire Quarter Sessions warned that 'communications will be stopped with the County of Dorset unless the work is immediately begun . . .'. A stone bridge was needed 'on account of the great weights carried over the bridge and the frequency, heighth and impetuosity of the floods'. It was rebuilt in that year, and the downstream arch still bears the inscription: 'Built by the County. G. Hookey. Mason 1784'.

Only eight years later the magistrates again complained: 'in great floods it is entirely impassable for Man, Horse or Carriage . . . notwithstanding it is one of the high Roads between Christchurch and Pool . . .'. Though repaired several times with timber piles, and partly rebuilt in 1843, Iford Bridge survived into the motor age only twelve feet wide. Traffic was controlled from a box at the Bournemouth end, by an RAC patrolman operating ropes to a semaphore arm. When a new bridge opened in 1933, the two eastward arches, which had been partly blocked, were rebuilt to match the original ones of 1784, and the old bridge has remained closed to motor traffic.

Most river crossings bring people to live at them. Sixty years ago the Iford Bridge Hotel was the New Inn; across the road was Harry Counter's shop and boathouse, while on the sloping bank now between the two bridges, were his tea-gardens. Lambert's, with a landing-stage, were downstream, where Clingan Road approaches the river. Clingan Farmhouse was opposite the New Inn, and the road to the new bridge in 1934 cut across the farm. West of it, where Bridle Crescent now runs, was Iford House with its gardens; only the coachhouse remains, under the name of Sheepwash Flats. Iford Farm lay on both sides of the road to Bournemouth, and the large dairy herd came down Water Lane twice a day to drink. Milk was supplied to shops in Boscombe, though in 1922 the Iford Farm Dairy Company started retail deliveries. Land along Iford Lane to the railway supplied garden produce by horse-drawn cart to regular customers in the town.

Iford's layout changed little before the new bridge was built with an altered road alignment, though thatched cottages in Water Lane and Old Bridge Road had gone already, and Harry Counter opened his Cara-Camp in the 1920s. At that date there were only some thirty houses in the little area of Iford.

The Stour, rising in Wiltshire, passes beneath its last bridge at Tuckton, though one was not built until 1883. The place was mentioned as Tuckton in the Christchurch Cartulary of 1407, and in a manor roll of 1412 as Touketon. Tuckton Lane led towards the farm in Iford Lane and on towards Wick, linked by a ford to Quomps at Christchurch.

A ferry was started about 1880 by Eli Miller, whose family kept it until 1903. The new ferryman then worked from 5.30 am to 11 pm, punting across for a halfpenny fare. A houseboat serving teas was moored on the Wick side, and in 1927 a holiday camp was built opposite. In September 1957 it seemed that the ferry was closed for ever, but new houses on the Wick side, and Pontin's at Christchurch, now keep Wick Ferry busy all season. Bright's *Guide* in 1888 advertised: 'Good boats may be obtained from 6d an hour at the Tuckton Bridge, and also at the Wick Ferry'. Outbuildings at Wick Farm, one bearing the date 1843 patterned in brick, were being converted late in 1984.

Hedwinesburh — the fort of Hedwine — is the imaginative name of Bournemouth's eastern headland. Maps of about 1600 show the name in its present form but, in the 19th century, ironstone that made and kept the Head was almost its own destruction. In the 1670s Andrew Yarraton had noticed a valuable ridge offshore — Beerpan Rocks — and in 1848 a Christchurch coal merchant, J. E. Holloway, formed the Hengistbury Mining Company to dredge it. The doggers of ore, rich in 30% iron, returned to South Wales as ballast in coal ships. Deprived of its natural protection, the Head quickly wore back; and although protests ended exploitation by 1870, the cliff eroded until the Council in 1939 built a groyne over 200 yards long. Holloway's Dock north of the Head had been cut for loading more ironstone from his quarry on Warren Hill.

Double Dykes is the site now in danger. Mackenzie's survey in 1784 showed the parallel ramparts curving south-east, but a 150-yard strip has since been lost. A plan in 1912 for eighty houses on the Head prompted the first serious dig of lowlands on the harbour side, where several Iron-Age and Roman items had been found; and ploughing in 1913 for an intended golf course turned up thousands of worked flints.

Now Bournemouth both values the Head's attractions and is concerned at them. From the top of Warren Hill the view extends east to Hurst Castle and the Isle of Wight, north towards Cranborne Chase and west along miles of beaches to the Purbeck ridge and Durlston Head. Nearby the Mudeford Spit crosses the Christchurch border to the Black House and the Run. Hundreds of leisure craft fill the shallow harbour where Iron-Age traders met two thousand years ago.

'Hengistbury Head belongs to Sir George Meyrick', explained an early *Guide to Southbourne*, 'who allows people to go there provided they keep to the beaten path and are without dogs'. He sold it before 1920, and soon Hengistbury was to have what its architect Philip Tilden called 'the largest castle in the world'. From Double Dykes to Mudeford Spit would be a cloistered garden, fountains, a Roman piazza before a domed hall of stairways, and a thousand-foot vista of saloons with views over terraces to the sea. Guests would find 250 suites of rooms, some of them in a tower over 200 feet high, which itself included studies, laboratories, observatories and a rooftop view over the Channel.

The castle would have its own quay, rising by steps through bastioned walls that lined the sea cliff with towers, balconies and rampart walks. For the many years all this was building, the owner would live in the Small Castle at the eastern end. Gordon Selfridge planned all this, and built none.

An American born in 1858, Selfridge had opened his London store in 1909 and now, with uncounted wealth, he planned a palace. But Warren Hill was as wild as he found it when in 1930 he sold the 700-acre Hengistbury Estate, Bournemouth buying the Head itself, 357 acres, for £25,250. Now the sea at Double Dykes and thousands of footsteps on the thin soil change it more than Gordon Selfridge ever did.

Winton has had a bad press — worse, hardly any. The standard histories of Bournemouth do not recognise Winton until it was given a parish council in 1894; though farther from the town centre, Pokesdown had been admitted by the Commissioners ten years before. Moordown had the respect of history, being named in Holdenhurst parish records in the 18th century, but Winton seems to have sprung onto the map as late as 1872.

Even the name is uncertain; probably it comes from the Talbot family whose relative, the Earl of Eglinton, was created Earl of Winton in 1859. The Bournemouth entry in that year's *Hampshire Directory* does not mention it, nor in 1867. Even in 1894, a guide published by the Town's Interest Association was not interested in Winton. No spacious villa in wooded grounds appeared there.

All this made little difference to the people of Winton, who had been settling unrecorded since mid-century in refuge from the high rents of Bournemouth. Until 1859 they even had to register their births, marriages and deaths at Christchurch. The way to the town they called the Richmond Hill Road, the Wimborne Road then being used (naturally enough), for the track connecting that town with Christchurch through Kinson and Iford — along the present Castle Lane.

Winton was noticed in 1868 by Throop's Congregational minister, who built a hall, the 'Pro Bono Publico', and next year Richmond Hill chapel set up a mission there. An Anglican school chapel, costing £359, had been built at Moordown in 1853, as St John's in the Wilderness, until a new St John's in 1874 cost £2,361 and became the parish church. At the other end of Winton, St Luke's was not dedicated until 1898.

East, to the Indian Hut where five ways met, lay Claypit Common where gipsies camped. Mark Loader won squatter's rights there in a lawsuit with the Earl of Malmesbury in 1906. Shorthorn Common extended south, to include land that later became Winton Recreation Grounds. A post office, opened in 1875, remained on the corner of the present Castle Road for almost a century. Winton Farm was opposite, with a heathland track to Withermoor. Ensbury Park Road was Muccleshell Lane, and Osborne (now Oswald) Road led to Redhill Common. Kinson parish register records the burial of 'William Hewes, a travelling huckster' who died in a tent there in 1867.

When White's *Hampshire Directory* found Winton in 1878 — and listed it as though it had no connection with Bournemouth — the street had at least seven shops as well as a wheelwright, blacksmith and builder. Brannon's 1871 *Bournemouth Guide* had noticed 'the rising village of Winton, which is becoming a populous suburb for the labouring population of Bournemouth'. Nine years later the *Guide* directed visitors to 'the Cemetery at Rush Corner, where the road turns sharply to the left and leads to the villages of Talbot, Winton and Moordown, which enliven the road by their appearance of neatness and comfort'. A *Penny Handbook* for Bournemouth in 1872 had described Winton as 'mostly built by and for artizans', and estimated 'nearly 1000 of the labouring classes'.

By 1890 St John's parish magazine was able to claim a 'unique attraction . . . in the affable style, disposition and arrangements of the working people's houses'. But there was 'no public form of any kind of entertainment, no proper cricket ground, the supply of drinking water terminates as though Peter's Hill was too much for it . . . a local committee supplies oil lamps etc.'. Cottages were being built for £240, with weekly rents of 4s 6d to 5s 6d. 'Perhaps,' remarked the parish magazine, 'there is no such other place in the world as Winton'.

On the second day of 1895 the parish council first met, at once urging the Gas and Water Company to extend supplies to Moordown. Next year Bournemouth Borough Council planned to enlarge its area to Talbot Village through the Malmesbury Planatations, (now Talbot Woods), adding about 300 acres which Mr Cooper Dean wished to drain for building development. The town clerk denied the town was trying to annexe potentially valuable land while leaving out Winton.

In their 1,237 acres lived at least 6,000 people, and between 1881-91 the number of houses had trebled. The parish council would have more power as an Urban District, though it would have to pay for lighting, scavenging and road-watering, and Moordown ward wished to secede to Holdenhurst parish. On 1 October 1898 Winton Urban District Council first met, soon asking for more police protection, and 'that measures be taken to suppress the prevalance of bad language'.

The new Council also asked the railway company to build a station near, or divert the line, but this was refused. Moordown's water supply was still poor, and had to be relieved by three daily carts. Cesspool emptying was expensive, and the sanitary committee recommended that 'disposal of household refuse be dealt with in a satisfactory way by the occupier'.

To Bournemouth Council, Winton was in fact a township. The Surveyor's department in 1900 wanted a tramway to the centre of Winton because it would 'tend to prevent the growth of congested or insanitary districts within the Borough as, provided the industrial classes can obtain cheap and rapid transport from their work, they have no longer any inducement to dwell near the centre of a town'. From 9 November 1901, only seven years since its parish council first met, Winton was to be in Bournemouth. When trams arrived in 1903, they ran to a depôt at Moordown. After 1906, houses filled the land of Malmesbury Farm at the end of Alma Road, and on the farmhouse site rose the Electric Palace, later the Winton Palace Theatre, boasting itself 'the only Place of Amusement in Winton'.

Winton public library was opened in 1907, and a travelling menagerie camped in fields behind as late as 1915. Four years later Winton Farm was still working. The 'parades' of shops lined the road to the Hollies, where John Lawford the bootmaker had planted holly bushes by his cottage gate. Winton had taken over Moordown where, a century before, the cottagers had looked for a white flag flown at Throop Congregational Church to announce that the minister was there.

Wherever land was enclosed, families found themselves barred from common grazing and fuel; only the efforts of William West had secured turbary for the Christchurch commoners. The wealthy Talbot sisters, Georgina Charlotte and Mary Anne, resolved to created a model village where the virtues of cleanliness, industry and gratitude would be practised. In 1835 they bought high ground between Ensbury and the county border towards Poole.

The 465 acres were enclosed, though 150 were kept as heathland for common use, and during 1850-62 the builder David Tuck laid out roads and plantations. In 1867 the estate was named Talbot Village, with local landed gentry as trustees. Besides six farms there were now a church, a school, and almshouses for fourteen labourers or small farmers. Most usefully, the Talbot sisters built nineteen pattern-book cottages which, though small and dark by today's standards, were far from the mud and thatch of many heath-dwellers. Altogether Talbot village was home for 126 people.

Each cottage was set in an acre of garden for vegetables and pigs; tenants could sell the produce, but not set up in trade. They had to conform to the trust's rules: 'The head of each household will be responsible for the good conduct and proper behaviour of the females'. No person was to be admitted from Hampshire.

The school was a single room nearly fifty-seven feet long, heated by one open fire. Starting with about sixty children, it had ninety-two admitted in 1902, and closed for a month for building a new infants' room. The headmaster in 1883 deplored the 'large percentage of dullards owing to low habits and home influence of parents . . . low standard of morality at Highmoor'. Its benefactors did not intend to be forgotten; their school was endowed with £66 'so long as the portrait of Georgina Charlotte shall hang in the Schoolroom'. She died in 1870, two years after laying the foundation stone of the church. No services were held after dark — 'very admirable in places having a good police, but no wise advisable in winter on a dark heath . . .'. A dark heath it remained into the 1950s, with surrounding land unbuilt. Land then lay empty southwards into Bourne Valley, Talbot Woods sheltered the village from the north, and Wallisdown was an outpost on the high road westwards.

Talbot Village once knew the day and hour by the church tower's mechanical chimes, which four times daily played a different hymn for each day of the week — until the works wore out. It was said that mechanical chimes were installed by Miss Mary Anne Talbot because she feared ringers might spend their pay at the Wallisdown pub. For many years before her death in 1890, aged 99, she attended church by carriage from High Wood House on the East Cliff. Her relative and heir Lord Leven built Talbot Boys' Home in her memory.

A few of the nineteen cottages have gone, with their half-crown rents, and farms have become school playing-fields. The largest, Talbot Village Farm, with 111 acres, is now partly the Dorset Institute of Higher Education. Talbot Farm, lately known as Slades after its last tenant, was only thirty acres and is now a housing estate. Others were even smaller: the farmhouses of White Farm and Lollipop remain, though their land is now Glenmoor School. Middle Farm is deserted, though Highmoor Farm is still worked; each was only fifteen acres. In spite of development, Talbot Village remains a Victorian island, where gardens still surround the cottages, and the pines of Talbot Woods protect church, school and almshouses from most modern sights.

Unlike other parts of the town, Westbourne grew quietly, with dignity and relative wealth. It was never a rival watering-place, like Boscombe, an innovation like Southbourne, or a township like Winton. The Commissioners' District from 1856 included part of Westbourne and reached most of the way to the Dorset border.

Branksome Tower had been built on the Dorset side in 1855. Its drive (The Avenue) met the Poole road on the border, where 'County Gates' of iron formed the entrance to the estate. The lodge was taken over by Rebbeck's in 1890, and survived until the 1960s. Adjoining the Hampshire side was Branksome Dene, begun in 1860, on over forty acres bought from Robert Kerley.

As a dower house to Branksome Dene, Alumhurst was built by 1863 and, then the Herbert Home, opened in 1867 as a sanatorium for convalescents. While Branksome Dene was owned by Lord Wimborne of Canford House, the Churchill family stayed there, and young Winston spent three days unconscious after falling from a bridge in Alum Chine.

This Branksome land, and more along the Poole Road owned by the Consolidated Land Society, had been part of the late Miss Bruce's estate, extending as far south as Bourne Bridge. By 1870 Seamoor House was one of four between Poole Road and Crescent Road, to which the house gave its present name of Seamoor Road. While living there, Henry Joy built Westbourne Arcade in 1884, with seats down the centre and racks for bicycles. It was guarded by a uniformed beadle with gold braid on his cap, who locked the main gates at night. The traders' association provides floral hanging baskets in summer. The Arcade at Westbourne remains the busiest of those in the town, since it forms a short cut between the two business streets and is itself full of small specialist shops. Its half-way bend allows both ends to be perpendicular to the streets and, by limiting the vista, makes itself seem longer. In fact it is safer to look at the floor, since tiles of different colours have worn unevenly.

By trying to be a miniature Bournemouth, Westbourne seems to retain some features of the nineteenth-century town. The street at the County Gates end of Seamoor Road was once even called the Square. A few yards away, the houses in roads leading south are small semi-detached villas a century old. When the Grand Super-Cinema was opened in December 1922, it had a revolving roof to admit pine-scented air, and the crews of Westbourne trams were said to be senior men chosen for their courtesy. It was naturally in Westbourne that in the 1970s a private garage was found to contain an Argyll tourer, made in 1908 and unused since the owner's death in 1916. The chauffeur, now aged eighty-six, found his cap on the car seat and put it on. Westbourne seems to demand a proper standard of dress.

It is unlikely that the character of Dr Jekyll (or Mr Hyde) was taken from anyone in Westbourne, though the author wrote the story while living there. Robert Louis Stevenson came to Bournemouth in 1884, and the following April moved into a house his father had bought in Alum Chine Road. He named it 'Skerryvore' after the lighthouse his family firm had built in Scotland. When Stevenson left there, it was on his final journey abroad to his death in Samoa in 1894. After severe air-raid damage in November 1940, the house was demolished and the site laid out as a memorial garden. Low walls outline the rooms where Stevenson lived, as he said, 'like a weevil in a biscuit', and where the adventure of *Kidnapped* came to life through his pen.

The isolation that Stevenson felt at Westbourne he could hardly have felt elsewhere. Today its centre remains two streets of shops (one-way since 1930), many long-established, linked by a Victorian arcade. Closing of the West Station and building of Wessex Way have increased its isolation. It is almost an oasis on the road to Poole. The small 'bus station that from 1932 to 1953 was a stop for the 'green buses' seemed like an outpost, for the unfamiliar roads of Poole lay beyond. 'County Gates' was a landmark; Westbourne, the end of Bournemouth.

When Kinson rang its church bell in 1812 it was for successes against Napoleon — not for the Tregonwells' arrival to live at Bourne. At the beginning of the century Kinson had 96 houses and a population of 497, when Bournemouth had the Decoy House. Half a century later, Kinson tything in the parish of Canford still had one and a half times as many people as the parish of Holdenhurst.

Kinson parish was enormous. In the sixteenth century it had stretched from the Stour in the north to the significantly-named Canford Cliffs in the south, and the town ditch of Poole. The track from that town to Longham bridge formed most of Kinson's western limits. The east was the Hampshire border — though so little importance was given to the coastal heath that Kinson (and Dorset) once encroached to the mouth of the Bourne. At the 1805 Enclosure the county border was at Durley Chine and, between 1811 and 1818, moved farther west to Alum Chine, where it stayed to 1974. The chapel of Kinson was in the far north, edging the Stour meadows, in the only farmed and fertile spot in the tything.

As settlers scattered the higher heathland, Kinson lost Parkstone in 1835 and Branksome in 1905, becoming a civil parish itself in 1895. By then Bournemouth was a Borough reaching to Redhill, only a mile from the centre of Kinson, where the parish council was aware of its comparatively limited powers in maintaining rights of way over the heath. As more people moved in to be near the town, farmers grew more concerned for their land, and landowners (such as Lord Leven, who had succeeded to the Talbot estate), thought of property values. Heathland tracks from West and East Howe, Wallisdown and Withermoor wandered over the heath on the edge of growing Bournemouth. Kinson people saw the town as an adventure, an exciting place for a day's shopping. Trams at Moordown in 1903 were only a half hour's walk from the village over Redhill Common.

Poole wanted Kinson, but the parish council voted unanimously to join Bournemouth in 1931. For the old village it was a tidying-up. Until a few years before, Kinson had received its post and its policing from Wimborne; it had been in Poole Poor Law Union, and the grammar school was there; the parish council in 1929 had noted with relief Bournemouth fire brigade's agreement to attend any fire in Kinson. Churches in the area adopted in 1931 stayed in the diocese of Salisbury, while the rest of Bournemouth is in Winchester.

Kinson land was now open to urban developers. Pitts Farmhouse, whose fields fronted Poole Lane and the Wimborne Road, was demolished about 1932, though until the 1950s, when the Council built large housing estates, the heathland remained a maze of tracks and gravel pits. Cudnell Farmhouse, occupied by the Elliott family from 1816 to 1956, went two years later; Durdells, south of Wimborne Road and almost opposite Cudnell, in 1970. Howe Lodge and Kinson House have vanished almost unnoticed, and a giant cedar near Avebury Avenue is all that marks the garden of lost Ensbury House.

The dignified Pelhams near Kinson Church dates from 1793, and is therefore, after the much-altered Stourfield House, the oldest mansion in Bournemouth. After almost ninety years as the vicarage, Pelhams was sold by Rev A. M. Sharp to the Council, on condition that it should be for community use and its land not built on. The land became a public park, and in 1952 the house was opened as Kinson Community Centre.

At the end of the lane beside Pelhams is Manor Farm (once Kinson Farm), close to the Stour and in a pastoral setting that contrasts with the main road only half a mile away. Southward from the Wimborne Road tracks climbed onto the heath. Poole Lane passed West Howe Farm on its way from Kinson Church and Longham bridge — the direct road past Bear Cross is not on old maps. Kinson Road led to the Congregational Chapel built in 1834, and still existing. Just east of the chapel lay East Howe Farm, on the track from Headless Cross — now East Howe Lane.

Until about 1840 the Royal Oak was the Travellers Rest, and travellers needed it. Brickmaking made thirst too, and it was the chief employer of the southern parish. Elliott's potteries, which for twenty years were near Bear Cross, moved to West Howe where better clay gave superior products, and continued to 1966. The corner of the parish up at Howe, between Ringwood and Wallisdown Roads, was Bankes Heath.

Until the 1950s, the old school in Kinson Road, at East Howe, seemed a fort defending Bournemouth. Then the Council filled the heath with housing estates, in which at least two dozen of the roads are named after war leaders and other servicemen. Kinson is the only part of Bournemouth to have grown from a village to a suburb, and so urbanised is it that motorists arriving in the town through Kinson have mistaken it for the town centre four miles beyond. Turbary Common towards Wallisdown is the only area of open land in the town that looks like the primal Bournemouth scene. Kinson has lost its pound for stray cattle, though it was given a village green in 1968. Only a few hundred Kinson people have lived there long enough to have changed counties twice.

Pines enclose St Mark's School at Talbot Village. (A)

Moordown and Winton, 1910: OS 6″ to one mile. Moordown began at Malvern Road, and part of Moordown Farm outbuildingsremained to 1978; though most of its land became the West Way estate in the 1930s. (DCL)

LEFT: Several thatched buildings remain in Kinson and Howe, which were taken into Bournemouth in 1931. Primrose Cottages stand in East Howe Lane. RIGHT: Boundary stone of land bought in 1835 by the Misses Talbot for their model village. It stands in Columbia Road. BELOW: Memorial plaque to R. L. Stevenson at Alum Chine. OPPOSITE ABOVE: Each in its acre of ground, Talbot Village cottages have stood since the 1860s. LEFT: Stourwood, one of Southbourne's early mansions. RIGHT: The Stourcliff estate was sold for housing in the 1890s, but its mansion remains in Ken Road. (All A) BELOW: In 1904 the Council bought Tuckton Bridge for £15,500, rebuilding it in reinforced concrete to carry trams. Trolleybus passengers bought a ½d toll ticket until 1942. (DCL)

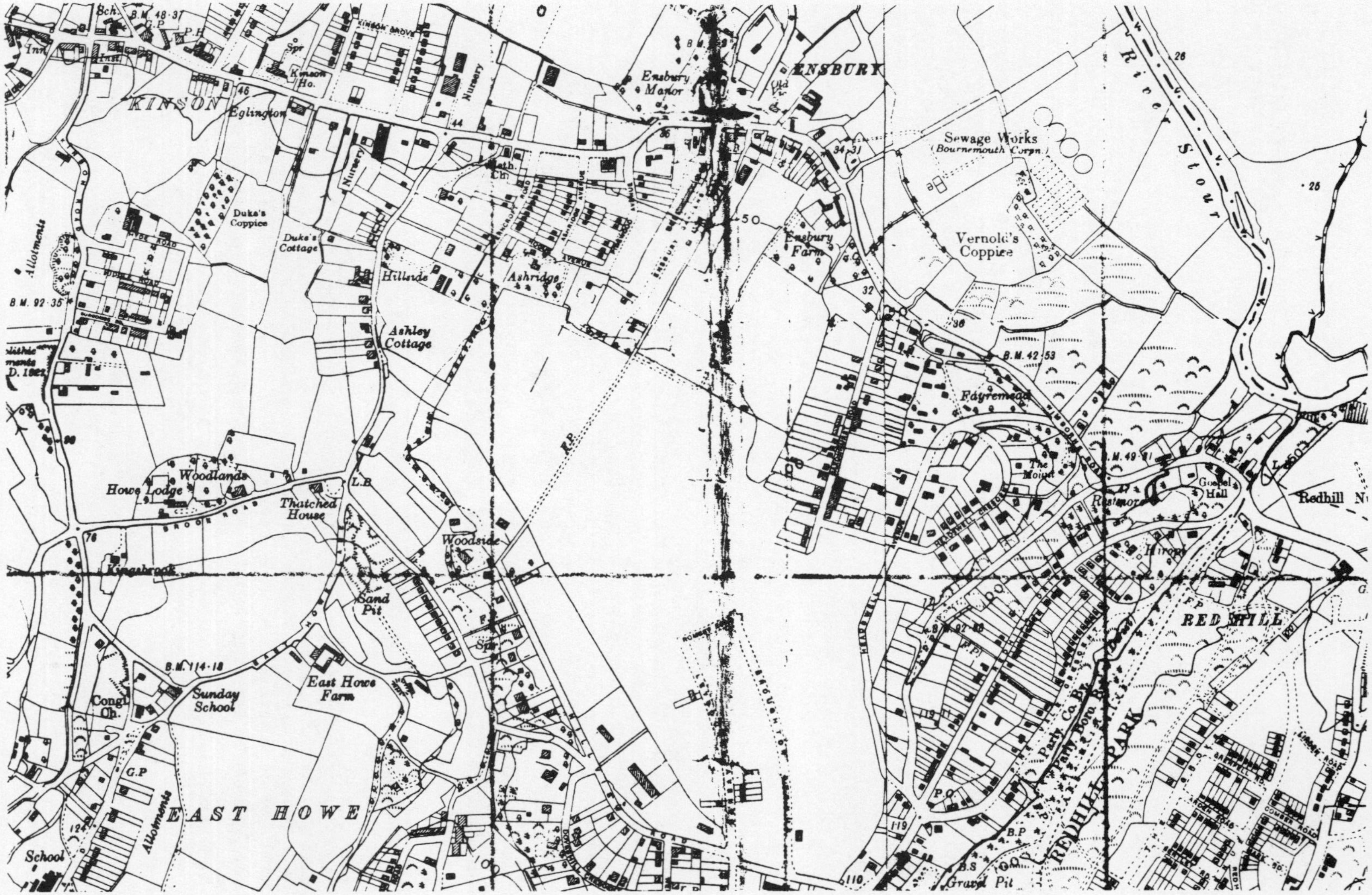

East Howe and Ensbury, 1932: OS 6″ to one mile. A year after Bournemouth's boundary extension, the county border is still shown at Redhill. Leybourne and Broughton Avenues are striking out across the former airfield at Ensbury Farm. (DCL)

ABOVE: Trams reached Winton in 1903. In the distance is Peter's Hill, with trees round St John's Church. BELOW: The toll-collector stands outside his cottage at the first Tuckton Bridge, built of timber for £4000 in 1883-83. (Both DCL)

ABOVE: Southbourne promenade (1885) and pier (1888) after storms of 1900-01. BELOW: 'The Square' at Westbourne. The corner shop is Williamson and Treadgold's; right is a cabmen's shelter. The tram route to Christchurch opened in 1905. (Both DCL)

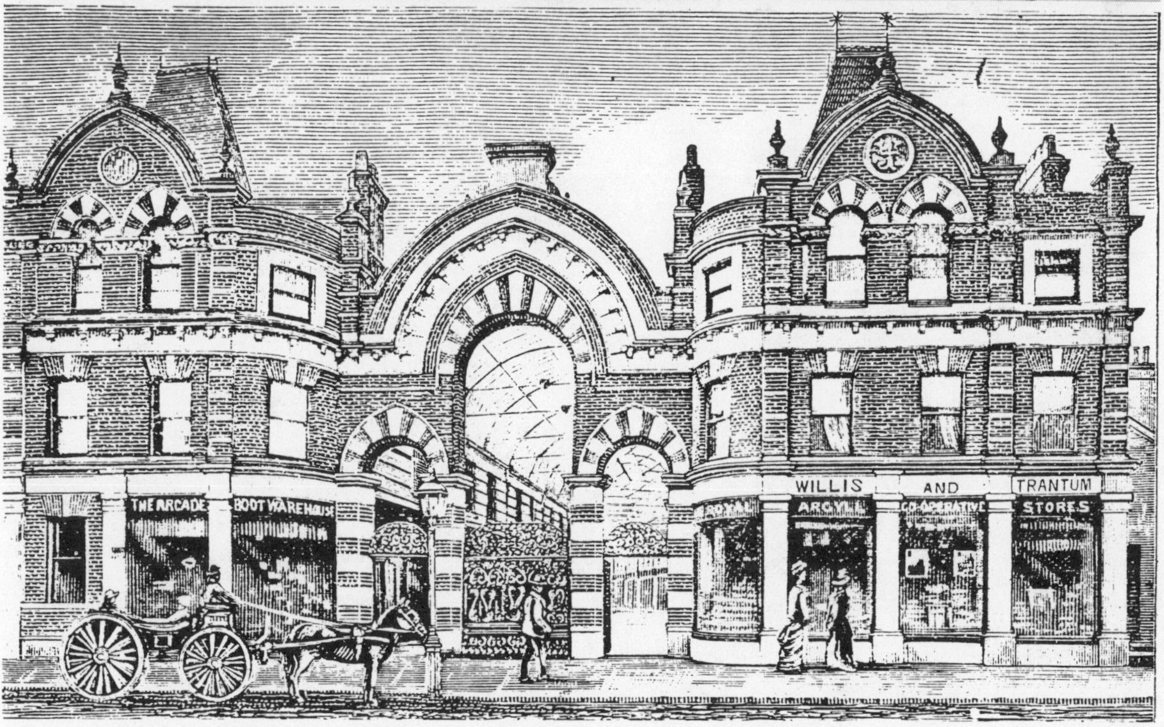

ABOVE: Southbourne promenade and sea wall, 1886-1902, with Dr Compton's terrace of Undercliff West. BELOW: In this 1886 print the Westbourne Arcade was two years old, built by Henry Joy who lived at Seamoor House nearby. (Both DCL)

Talbot Village and Winton, 1903. 6″ to one mile. Talbot Village cottages line the road to Wallisdown; handwritten notes refer to archaeological finds. (DCL)

Towers Among the Trees

'From the way the churches are thronged,' wrote Grantley Berkeley in 1865, 'and the frequency of Divine Service, I had thought at first that Bournemouth must rank high in sancitity and decorum, but on inspecting the visitors' list kept at the Library, I therein saw that no less than twenty-seven clergymen had arrived in one week. What means this advent of religious men?'

It had been different in 1838, when two cottages west of the Bridge made an improvised church. Dr Granville may not even have noticed it when he advised that 'a plain, unassuming and well-built rural church . . . should be erected near the entrance to the park'. Seven months after his visit, on 28 September 1841, in just such a spot, the foundation stone of St Peter's Church was laid.

Next year Sydenham's *Guide* noted that it would be 'A small, neat structure . . . free from any superfluous ornament . . . at the sole expense of the wealthy baronet'. But when, a few months later, Sir George Gervis died, the Chancery Court had to arrange for competition and endowment. At its opening in 1845 it was already too small; 150 sat in a church 76 by 26 feet, and 90 more in a gallery, where a band led the music.

That year Rev Alexander Morden Bennett arrived to take charge of St Peter's District, extending from the Dorset border to Boscombe and north almost to Moordown. The endowment was only £50 a year, with pew-rents and a parsonage house. First extension was a south aisle and vestry in 1851, and two years later Morden Bennett began a quarter-century's association with G. E. Street as architect. He planned a north aisle in 1853, and by 1860 the roof was raised by a clerestory that gave 'all height and no length'. At once Street planned transepts leading from a chancel beyond a high arch, and all these were finished by 1864.

Morden Bennett favoured a Tractarian or Ritualist form of worship, which then aroused controversy and even conflict with the law. John Keble, who worshipped at St Peter's just before his death in 1866, was a High Church pioneer. In 1868 the Bishop forbade candles except for necessary lighting. For Evangelical worship Holy Trinity was opened in 1869, but St Clement's in 1873 on 'Boscombe Heath' was even more Ritualist than St Peter's, with men and women sitting on opposite sides. Two years later the Convent of the Sisters of Bethany settled next to St Clement's.

Near the West Cliff, in 1866 G. E. Street built a temporary church dedicated to St Michael, which left only its name to the road, when a permanent church was begun in Poole Road in 1874 by Street's pupil, Norman Shaw. For the wealthy East Cliff area the same architect in 1876 built St Swithun's, still in St Peter's parish.

Morden Bennett had not forgotten the parish beyond the town. His appeal for a chapel at the Moordown mission school in 1853 raised £359 to build St John in the Wilderness — the wilderness being that of the Baptist as well as of Moordown. Street's first work in Bournemouth is now a builders' merchants' showroom. He began another mission school with a church (St James) at Pokesdown in 1858. Both these, and St Swithun's, were on land given by Sir George Meyrick.

'One of the grandest structures in the South of England', would be St Peter's, said Morden Bennett, if it had the tower designed by Street in 1853. It was added in 1869-70, with six bells dedicated in 1871. For three years the tower remained detached twenty feet from the church. In 1879 an 86-foot spire made St Peter's over two hundred feet high. A month after the service of thanksgiving, Morden Bennett died (in January 1880), but his church was complete.

Roman Catholics until 1862 found their nearest church at Poole, travelling by hired horse-bus in summer. Several wintering families set up private oratories in Bournemouth to which visitors were invited. In 1869 two priests opened a chapel in Branksome Wood Road, and next year a wooden chapel for ninety worshippers was used at Richmond Hill. There the Oratory of the Sacred Heart was built in 1873-75, and rebuilt on the same site in 1896-1900, when Corpus Christi Church opened at Boscombe.

Besides G. E. Street and Norman Shaw, several other nationally-known architects built in Bournemouth. The Annunciation Church in Charminster Road was Sir Giles Gilbert Scott's work in 1906, and St Augustin's was Butterfield's last church.

A Congregational chapel of 1834 remains at East Howe, though churches adjoining are now used for worship, and Throop chapel is earlier. 'A Meeting House for a congregation of Independent Dissenters' was on Poole Hill in 1849. Ten years later, Richmond Hill Congregational Church was opened on land given by George Durrant, and rebuilt in 1891. For almost forty years until 1937 its minister was J. D. Jones, one of the town's most respected men. A Congregational chapel had opened at Pokesdown in 1858.

Wesleyan Methodists met in Orchard Street off Poole Hil in 1859, and a chapel opened in 1867 next to the Tregonwell Arms. From the sale of the site in 1886, the Methodists built the Punshon Memorial Church, named after a preacher and missionary. Prominent on Richmond Hill, it was badly damaged in an air raid on 23 May 1943, and a new church opened in Exeter Road in 1953.

At the foot of Richmond Hill the 'Scotch Church' appears in early photographs. The first building there from 1857 was of iron, lasting fifteen years until rebuilt in stone. In 1886 a new site across the Square was bought for the church — known as St Andrew's Presbyterian Church of England. Its spire, unsafe through war damage, was removed in 1947.

Near the Lansdowne, a Baptist chapel was begun in 1875. At Westbourne the West Cliff Tabernacle opened in 1891, followed by the Congregationalists (1898) and the Wesleyans (1899). In West Cliff Road a new St Ambrose was dedicated in 1900, and Christ Church in Alumhurst Road began in 1913.

In Holdenhurst Road in 1879, East Cliff Congregational stood at the edge of East Common, where its clock is still kept a minute fast to encourage railway passengers. St Paul's nearby came two years later, though St Mary's a mile farther out was not built until 1926. Charminster Road Congregational began in 1901, six years before the Roman Catholic Annunciation Church and seven before St Alban's — all three within five minutes' walk. Not far away a Wesleyan church opened in Alma Road in 1906.

As a memorial to Morden Bennett of St Peter's, a new Anglican church of St Stephen was opened in 1885. Architect J. L. Pearson had just begun Truro Cathedral, and the design of St Stephen's is the most impressive in the town, although the intended spire was not built.

Anglican churches followed the fast growth of the town — St John's in Surrey Road in 1889, St Andrew's in Malmesbury Park and St Augustin's nearby, both in 1892, St John's at Boscombe in 1895. As outer parts of the town filled, Congregational churches were founded at Pokesdown, (Immanuel church, 1910, moved after two years to the Carbery estate), and at Iford in 1933, near St Saviour's of 1936. When land towards Hengistbury Head was built on,

St Nicholas opened in 1961 as daughter church of St Katherine at Southbourne. Other post-war churches have been Holy Epiphany in Castle Lane, St Thomas at Ensbury Park and St Philip's at Kinson, a mile from old St Andrew's — the only mediaeval church in Bournemouth. St Barnabas, built on the Haddon Hill estate, is linked with Holdenhurst, the original parish church of Bournemouth. The Salvation Army built a new Citadel in 1984 at Boscombe, near their 1899 site.

The churches and chapels of Bournemouth are waymarks through the town. St Peter's seems to preside over the business centre, on eye level with Beales' restaurant. St Stephen's by the Town Hall looks like a cathedral, a spiritual seat of local government. St Clement's assertive tower of 1893, seen from the far perspective of Lowther Road, might be a mediaeval abbey. The only hilltop site is that of the romanesque St Francis, whose whitened tower has looked out from the town's northern bluffs since 1930. Ten minutes' walk away is the modest Deutsche Evangelishe Kirche in Malvern Road.

Others too are a surprise — the sudden spire of St John's among the trees of Surrey Road; the severe Mormon Church of Latter Day Saints next to the homely St Augustin's, and the spiky Punshon Memorial Church close to the pier. St Edmund Campion in Castle Lane looks as if it belongs to the Hampshire Centre. Within fifty yards of Old Christchurch Road are an Orthodox Jewish Synagogue and a Particular Baptist Chapel.

A Bournemouth vicar remarked in 1980 that 27 Anglican churches were 'too many'. Already Holy Trinity had been closed in 1973, converted to 'King Arthur's' banqueting hall, burned down in 1979, and its tower demolished in 1981. New roads and redevelopment isolated St Paul's, which held its last service on 20 July 1984 and was gone six months later, its work transferred to a new St Paul's on Throop housing estates. United Reformed churches at Charminster and Winton have been demolished, to be merged or rebuilt. Most denominations will have to consider the future of their less-used buildings, many on valuable sites, whose upkeep can be put to better purposes.

No Bishop of Bournemouth yet exists, though south-east Dorset with more than half a million people could form a new Anglican diocese. At present it is shared between Winchester and Salisbury, and the historic church of Wimborne Minister or Christchurch Priory could become a bishop's see.

LEFT: The Misses Talbot built St Mark's church in 1868 at Talbot Village, described in this 1893 print as 'a model Dorsetshire village out upon the moorlands'. RIGHT: St Michael's Church in Poole Road, designed by Norman Shaw, appears in this 1886 print ten years after opening. A tower was added in 1901. (Both DCL)

ABOVE LEFT: One of the town's most impressive church towers, added to St Clement's in 1893. (A) RIGHT: The tower and spire in this architect's drawing have not been added to St Alban's Church, built in 1908 on a site above Charminster Road. BELOW LEFT: St Paul's Church was consecrated in 1881. The spire that replaced this tower roof was removed in 1963 after storm damage, and the church closed in 1984. RIGHT: East Cliff Congregational (now United Reformed) Church was opened in Holdenhurst Road in 1979, and remains little affected by the redevelopment around it. (All DCL)

LEFT: The Punshon Memorial (Wesleyan) Church opened in 1886 at Richmond Hill, and badly damaged in an air raid on 23 May 1943. A new church was built in Exeter Road in 1954-58. (DCL) RIGHT: Now United Reformed, St Andrew's was built in 1887, and the 90-foot spire, on an 80-foot tower, was found to be bomb-damanged and removed in 1947. (DCL) BELOW: Town centre from the north-west in 1978, with St Michael's church in the centre. (Aerial photography by Ken Hoskin of Kitchenham Ltd.)

ABOVE: Holy Trinity in Old Christchurch Road. (DCL) LEFT: St Peter's Church, after a quarter-century of work by the architect G. E. Street, was completed with a spire in 1879. RIGHT: St Stephen's Church, designed by J. L. Pearson, was opened in 1885. The tower was finished in 1903 but the spire has not been added. (Both DCL)

Band to Radio

'At Bournemouth a man has no amusement of any kind . . . no association, no promenade . . .'. Writing his *Memories and Music* in 1924, Sir Dan Godfrey was quoting a comment of half a century before.

The town's first public music was the Italian Band, which came for a winter season in 1876 and stayed for sixteen years. They wore Italian army uniform, in which all had served, entertaining on the paddle-steamers and giving subscription concerts. They often played from a gallery over the Gervis Road end of the Arcade. In 1892 the town established the country's first Corporation military band, of twenty-one players under Signor Bertini.

Next year, the Corporation took over the Winter Gardens lease, appointing a musical director. He was Dan Godfrey, who quickly overcame his disadvantages of being only twenty-five and not having a foreign name. His orchestra of thirty players, now with a string section, gave their opening performance on 22 May 1893 to over five thousand at the Winter Gardens. Next year Dan Godfrey was appointed resident musical director of the first permanent municipal orchestra in Britain. It was not the town's only public music. Councillors reported in 1903 after visiting other resorts that Bournemouth should enjoy 'bands of music in the open air without the objectionable accompaniment of collecting boxes, to fill which visitors are importuned to their annoyance'. The orchestra's size was increased, until by 1910 the total annual cost was £8,600, excluding Dan Godfrey's salary. He was knighted in 1922, and gave his farewell concert in 1934.

When the orchestra moved to the new Pavilion in 1929, the Winter Gardens briefly became again a centre for popular amusements, until demolition began in November 1935. Two years later a new £30,000 building opened as an indoor bowling green — a function which accounts for its square plan. After wartime use by the Services, the Winter Gardens became a concert hall in October 1947, the home of the enlarged Municipal Orchestra of 47 under Rudolf Schwarz. Seven years later, when the Council voted against bearing the whole cost, an appeal fund supported it until a limited company, the Western Orchestral Society, took over with local and Arts Council support. The renamed Bournemouth Symphony Orchestra gave its first concert on 7 October 1954. Charles Groves remained as resident conductor, succeeded by Constantin Sylvestri.

Since then its financial uncertainties have often contrasted with its reputation. The orchestra has undertaken many tours abroad, and made many recordings. In 1968 the Bournemouth Sinfonietta was formed for smaller-scale performances.

Before any public theatre in Bournemouth, Sir Percy Shelley built a stage in his garden at Boscombe Manor, and later attached one to the house. On 26 December 1852 during performance of *A wreck ashore*, the *William Glen Anderson* drove ashore nearby and an unconscious sailor was revived at the Manor. The Bournemouth Amateur Dramatic Society began in 1876, and Sir Percy was later President.

'A handsome and well-appointed theatre' opened in the town on 7 December 1882. The Theatre Royal in Albert Road cost £10,000 and seated 800. Its manager was Harry Nash, who had already brought concerts to the Victoria Library in the Square, had published the *Bournemouth Observer*, and now carried on a stationery and printing business opposite the Arcade. Readings, contemporary drama, pantomime and the D'Oyly Carte Opera Company attracted large audiences, though serious opera, Shakespeare and lectures had few — except when Oscar Wilde made two appearances in 1883. Bournemouth people flocked to a Charles Hawtrey comedy, implied a reviewer, since it gave them 'the maximum of mirth with a minimum of thought'.

In 1887 the theatre was refitted as the New Town Hall, on hire for balls, banquets and bazaars, until in 1892 it was converted to the Bournemouth Theatre and Opera House with 1,100 seats. Four years later, Harry Nash's widow sold it to Morell and Mouillot, owners of many theatres and touring companies. Years of elaborate and popular productions followed, with colourfully printed programmes.

At Boscombe in 1900 Morell and Mouillot bought the theatre built fifteen years before by Archibald Beckett as part of his Royal Arcade scheme; he had aimed to attract audiences from working-class areas nearby, with prices less than half those of the town centre. Beckett withdrew in 1898 and, after two uncertain years, the Morell-Mouillot purchase gave it productions comparable with those at Albert Road. In 1905 it became a music hall, the Boscombe Hippodrome, with boxes at 15s and gallery for 3d.

The Theatre Royal was advertised in 1913 as 'possessing the most luxuriously fitted foyer in the country', but its location in a narrow commercial street could not rival the new Pavilion that rose above the gardens. After Mouillot's death in 1911, his widow managed the theatre until its lease expired in April 1939. During the war it was a Services' club, damaged by fire in October 1943. It reopened in June 1949 as the New Royal Theatre, until the proprietor's death in 1957. Two years later it was an opera house, in 1962 a cinema, and next year a bingo hall. In 1971 it reopened as the Tatler Cinema Club but, at its centenary in 1982, was empty, derelict and — remembering the happiness it had given to so many — the saddest building in Bournemouth.

In the 1930s Westover Road became established as the town's entertainment centre, with the new Pavilion and Regent and rebuilt Westover. In 1931 the Little Theatre opened there; though it was renamed the Palace Court Theatre four years later, its old name survives in the Little Theatre Club.

Early cinema scenes flicker across the years. In 1902 Edison's Electric Animated Pictures were showing a programme of Boer War films at the Grand Theatre (later Hippodrome) in Boscombe. West and Co were at the Shaftesbury Hall, and next year West's Pictures advertised a three-week return visit. For June 1910 West's had a programme of eleven films, some only a minute long, with an interlude of songs. The same year the Lansdowne Cinematograph Hall opened at 197 Old Christchurch Road, and was there at least till outbreak of war. The 1911 directory lists a bioscope theatre in Bourne Avenue.

In 'artisan' parts of the town the Coronation Picture Theatre (later Roxy) opened at Springbourne in 1911, and the Electric Picture Palace Picture House (later Plaza and now Continental) on 4 July 1912. Two more began about 1914 — the Clarence in the former Pokesdown Art and Technical School, and the Boscombe Cinema in Palmerston Road. The Boscombe New Picture House (later the Savoy) followed. In 1919 the Palladium opened at Fisherman's Walk, while the Westover rink and dance hall was then showing films.

Now cinemas were built on a new scale. The Electric, opened in Commercial Road in 1910, was transformed eleven years later to 'The Pleasure Palace of Bournemouth', with musical teas, when trays were clipped to seat-backs — 'comfortable lounge chairs a speciality' — and a roof tea-garden. Children's Special matinées were at three on Saturdays — 'two hours' continuous amusement . . . Amusing and Instructive Pictures will be given during these hours' — for twopence. Next year at Westbourne the Grand Super Cinema opened, with a sliding roof above its thousand seats.

Ninety-year-old villas came down in Westover Road for the Regent Theatre, opened on 13 May 1929. It was a magnificence new to the town, with an entrance hall ninety feet by thirty paved in black and white marble, and 'a very rich dado of Algerian onyx'. The style was said to be Italian Renaissance. Café-restaurant and lounges were open twelve hours a day, and nearly four hundred could admire, through the Regent's arcaded loggia, the Pavilion completed two months before. Above the 2,000 seats was an eighty-feet dome, and the souvenir programme assured that 'for the nervous patron, the cinema has twelve exits'. Reginald Foort rose at the Wurlitzer organ.

Talking pictures brought new prosperity, when at Boscombe the Astoria and Carlton opened. The Moderne, 'Bournemouth's latest wonder cinema', costing £70,000 in 1935, overshadowed the little Ritz at Moordown. Opened in 1936 in Albert Road near the Theatre Royal, the Premier News Theatre gave a 75-minute programme continuously from 11 am.

The Earl of Malmesbury in 1937 opened the last super-cinema, the Odeon near the Lansdowne. When wartime Sunday performances came, the town had fourteen cinemas. Evacuation, billeting, blackout and boredom filled them; until television in the 1950s, patrons expected to queue. Then came the closures, from the Ritz in 1959 to the Odeon in 1974. The Regent, renamed the Gaumont in 1949, continued before conversion to two cinemas with a large terrace bar in 1968; the Westover became the ABC, with three. Others were converted to stores; the Odeon, Moderne, Astoria and Grand offered bingo. Business premises now occupy the Boscombe Cinema Picture Palace of 1913, becoming the New Scala, in 1939 the Arcadia Funland, and next year a Palais de Danse. It was best known till the mid-fifties as the Boscombe Palais.

'The Sun never sets on West's Pictures' — it was bombed twice. An early programme included *The Rabbit Industry in Victoria*, and emigrants would have found T. J. West's company in Australia.

'Among the essentials of a watering place, a Library and News Room', announced Sydenham's *Guide* in 1840, 'forms a choice promenade for the lounger, whilst a plentiful supply of books, magazines, and newspapers, proffers information as to the course of a busy world, and presents sources of intellectual amusement and intelligence'. It was Sydenham's own library near the Belle Vue, and still the only one in 1867. 'The libraries of the town are numerous and well stocked', by 1894, when private ones were popular. But in the previous year the ratepayers had voted to adopt the Public Libraries Act, which allowed expenditure of a penny rate.

On the first day of 1895 a temporary library opened at 6 Cumnor Terrace, Old Christchurch Road. It was one of the first to adopt open access, 'which gives borrowers the privilege of handling the books and selecting them from the shelves'. A branch opened the same day near Boscombe Arcade. In 1901 the Bournemouth Free Library moved to 2 Stanhope Gardens — a house in Dean Park Road now named Old Library House. It still awaited its own premises, while in succession Winton, Springbourne, Boscombe and Westbourne buildings opened, all due to the American philanthropist Andrew Carnegie. Other gifts were the John Camm music library in 1910, and in 1969 the collection of W. J. Day, son of the town's first photographer, Robert Day.

In early years hours were long: lending and reference departments opened from 11 am to 9 pm, the newsroom 9 am to 10 pm. As demands on library services have increased, opening hours have incongruously shortened. Travelling libraries had served outlying parts in 1898, and permanent buildings followed — Charminster in 1932, and replacements for Boscombe, East Howe and Kinson. The first Library had moved from Dean Park Road in 1913 to the new Municipal College site at the Lansdowne, where it remains without enlargement. In 1974 it became the East Area headquarters of the Dorset County Library.

Bournemouth is a museum, it has been unkindly said. The Russell-Cotes has even been called a museum of museums where, walking from morning-room to dining-room to drawing-room, one can imagine the family at home in East Cliff Hall, which Merton Russell-Cotes built in his hotel garden. One can imagine how proudly he surveyed the town he helped to make, surrounded by the collection he gave to its people. Perhaps he would have wondered at the British Typewriter Museum's 350 models housed nearby; or at the Casa Magni at Shelley Park, home of the poet's son, with its collection of mementoes.

Newspapers cover most of Bournemouth's history. In the 18th century the *Salisbury and Winchester Journal* circulated in neighbouring towns, and the *Dorset County Chronicle* began in 1824. Later the *Poole and Dorset Herald*, as well as the *Christchurch Times*, carried reports on events at distant Bourne.

William Mate founded the first paper in the new town, though no copies are known from its first ten years; the earliest on Library microfilm is 1868. As the *Bournemouth Visitors' Directory* it printed weekly lists of new arrivals, as well as residents. The *Bournemouth Observer* published from 1875 to 1908, and the *Bournemouth Guardian* from 1883 to 1928. The *Bournemouth Graphic* published in 1902 on a superior paper for 2d, with photographs, surviving to 1935.

In 1919, after half a century the *Visitors' Directory* became the *Bournemouth Times*, which in turn became a free newspaper, the *Advertiser*, in 1982. The *Bournemouth Daily Echo* started in 1900, and is still published daily as the *Evening Echo*. The first office had been at Shaftesbury Chambers in Fir Vale Road, moving in 1909 to Albert Road, where the *Bournemouth Observer* had just ceased publication. In 1921 the *Echo* took over old bank premises opposite the Arcade. All offices moved to Richmond Hill in January 1934, in a new building designed not to look like a works. A commemorative article claimed it had 'more glass than any business building in Bournemouth' and its consumption of gas was 'large enough to maintain a liberal supply to a village the size of Broadstone'.

A pavilion such as Ferrey had planned in 1836 took almost a century in building. It needed Sir George Meyrick's permanent lease and his consent, and then the Bournemouth Improvement Act of 1892. Two years later, a design competition attracted five entries, and in 1901 Russell-Cotes persuaded the Council to approve the Belle Vue site. In 1922 they invited new plans for a £100,000 building, and one was chosen from 92 competitors. On 19 March 1929 the Pavilion was opened by the Duke of Gloucester. It had cost a quarter of a million pounds, and Alderman Cartwright, who had condemned opponents' claims of £200,000 as 'preposterous' was elected Freeman of the Borough.

To some the new Pavilion was a monstrosity that squandered the best site in Bournemouth. Others remember the Lucullus Restaurant, tea dances and the ballroom that flourished in the 1930s. Summer air from the sea and gardens filled it; in winter its warm corridors, smelling strongly of rubber flooring, half-encircled the auditorium. There the pantomime season began on Boxing Day and for children carried Christmas into February.

But new styles in entertainment, different tastes in catering and accommodation, perhaps more active leisure — all have undermined such a huge monument to the 1920s. After half a century the Pavilion's losses provoked ideas for new uses — an amusement or sports centre, a children's summer fun palace, or leasing off parts of the building for private schemes. The new Bournemouth International Centre of 1984 is the Pavilion's young rival — though significantly, under the same management.

Early experiments in wireless messages were made by Marconi from Madeira House west of the pier, with an aerial in the garden. A signal received here from Alum Bay, Isle of Wight in 1898 was the world's first paid wireless message. In the early 1920s he was working from the Haven Hotel at Sandbanks, and his yacht *Electra* often moored off Brownsea. All then was so experimental that developments were rapid. In September 1922 a Bournemouth School of Wireless began at 20 Lansdowne Road, and three months later the Bournemouth and District Radio and Electrical Society was formed. By the middle of 1923 Wireless Notes in the local press announced local broadcasting as imminent.

On 17 October 1923 the eighth provincial station of the British Broadcasting Company, 6BM, opened with two and a half hours of music and talks. Bournemouth people listened to loudspeakers in the Square and Arcade, from a car at the pier, at several business premises, and in their homes. First with advertising was Brights store, offering sets from 7s 6d to five guineas, and Beales warned of unsatisfactory apparatus. Twenty other Bournemouth firms joined in the sales.

The studios were on upper floors of Vernall's buildings in Holdenhurst Road. Two miles away in Bushey Road, Charminster, stood transmitting huts and two 120-feet masts, 200 feet apart. On a wavelength of 385 metres the Bournemouth station expected a 25-mile range. By the second week it was broadcasting three hours daily of local programmes, with over four hours to 11 pm relayed from London. Three local schools asked for wireless apparatus rooms, to be used only in the evenings, so that entertainment should not interfere with education.

Three years later 6BM was broadcasting from the Royal Bath, the Winter Gardens, Beales Restaurant and two cinemas. But in 1927 the new British Broadcasting Corporation's transmitter at Daventry reduced the output of small stations to local topics. When the Start Point transmitter opened on 14 June 1939, 6BM, once described by John Reith as the brightest jewel in the crown, closed down. In August the BBC opened a studio in Majestic Chambers in Westover Road, and local music was broadcast into 1942. As an anti-invasion measure, local transmitters were set up, and an aerial was strung to one of the refuse destructor chimneys, where the BBC still uses the site.

On the last day of December 1970, Radio Solent started regular programmes from its Rowridge transmitter on the Isle of Wight. With a reception area concentrated on Southampton and Portsmouth, Bournemouth has only a small share of its local coverage. But the town again had its own transmitter on 15 September 1980, when the commercial Two Counties Radio began. 2CR's premises are five minutes' walk from the former 6BM studio.

An 1878 engraving shows the skating rink and Winter Gardens Pavilion soon after opening. (DCL)

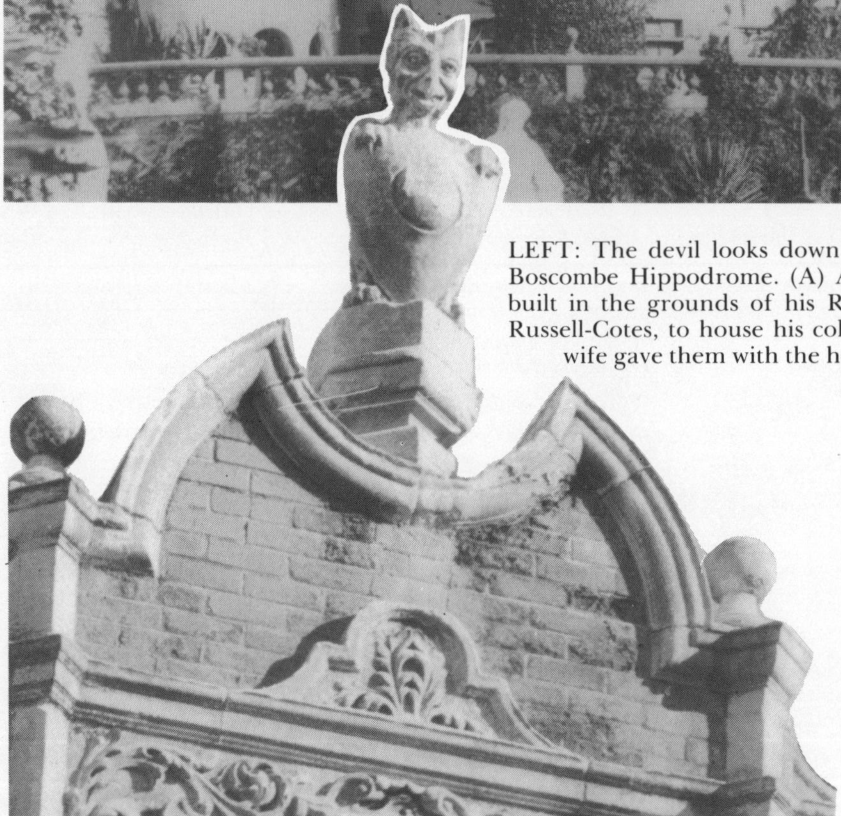

LEFT: The devil looks down over Christchurch Road to Boscombe Hippodrome. (A) ABOVE: East Cliff Hall was built in the grounds of his Royal Bath Hotel by Merton Russell-Cotes, to house his collections. In 1907 he and his wife gave them with the house to the town. (DCL)

ABOVE: Musicians mustered for a British Concert as part of the 1910 Centenary celebrations. Left to right, standing — Sir Edward German, Sir Hubert Parry (born in Bournemouth in 1848); seated — Sir Edward Elgar, Dan Godfrey (Director of Music, knighted 1922), Sir Alexander Mackenzie and Sir Charles Stanford. BELOW: The arcaded Regent Cinema (now Gaumont) faces the Pavilion forecourt; both buildings opened in 1929. (Both DCL)

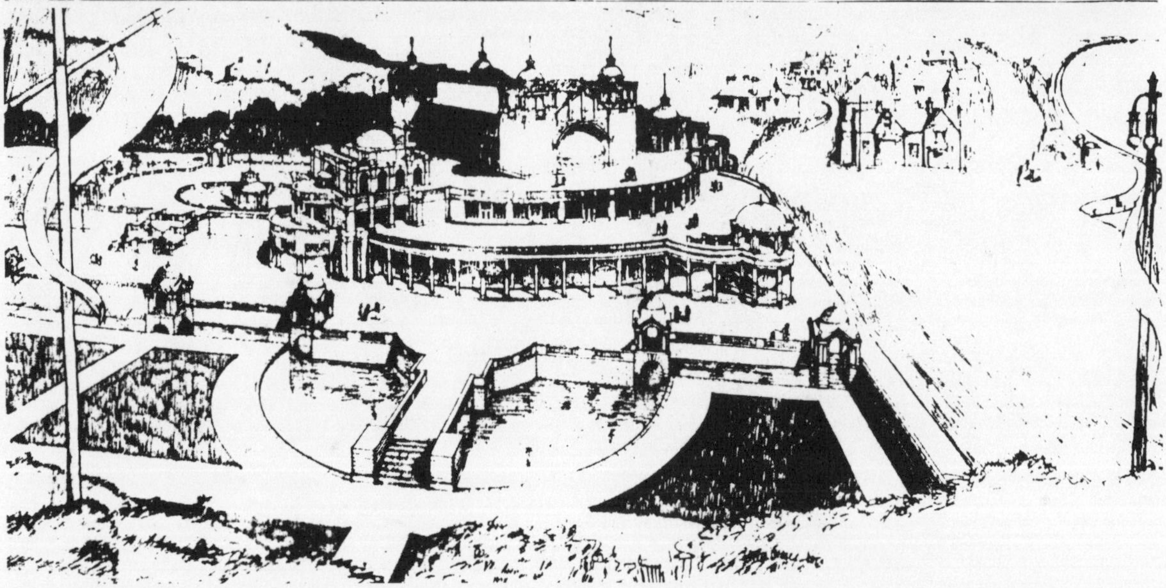

ABOVE: Winter Gardens in 1886. 'A comfortable lounge . . . kept at an even temperature of 60 deg. Open daily from 10 a.m. Admission (ordinary) Sixpence. Newspapers, as published, will be found in the Reading Room. Chess, Draughts, and other games . . .' BELOW: The present Pavilion was opened twenty years after this design appeared in the *Bournemouth Graphic* on 15 April 1909. (Both DCL)

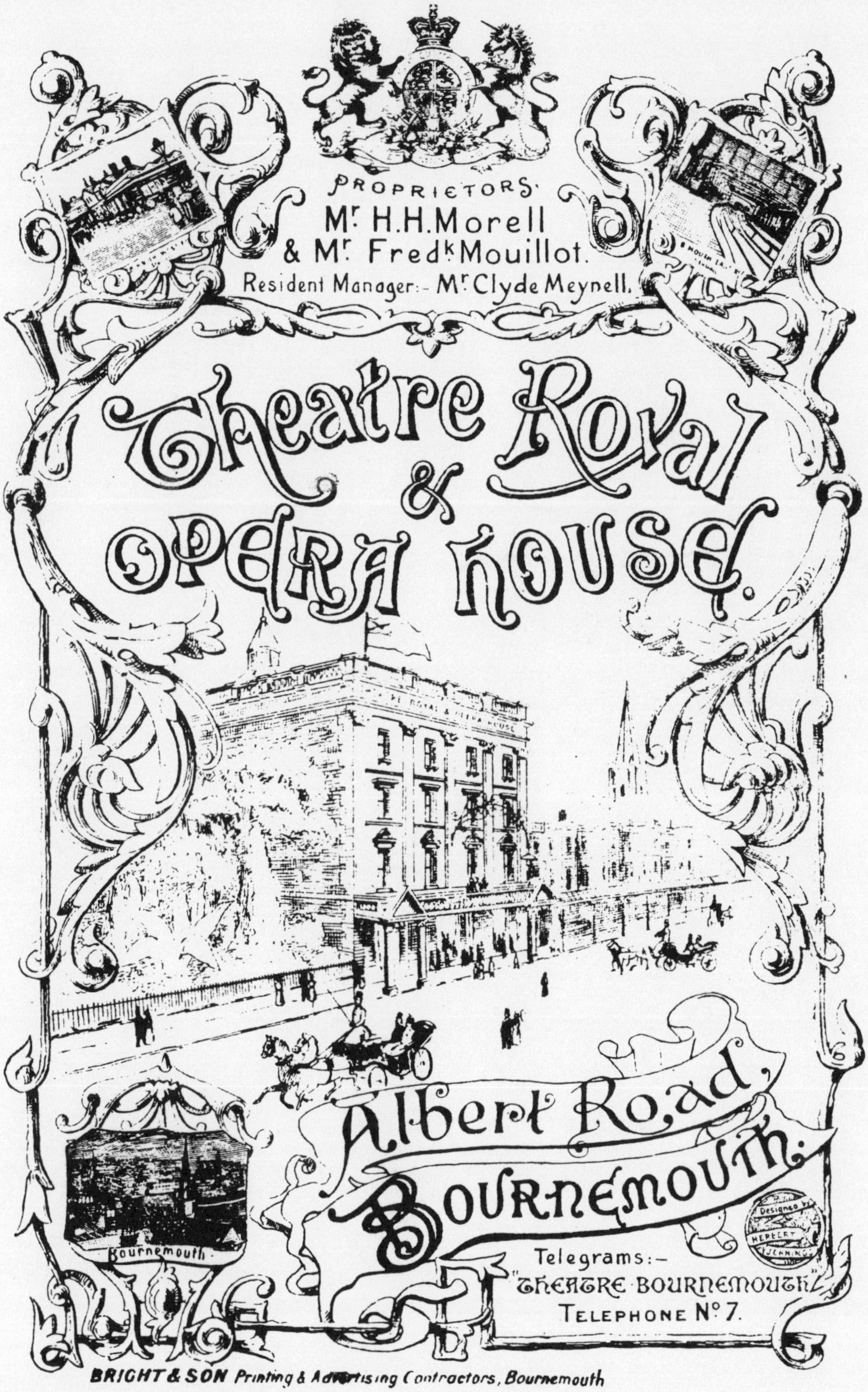

A programme of 24 September 1897 shows the Theatre Royal in its heyday, though Albert Road was never as wide as this. (DCL)

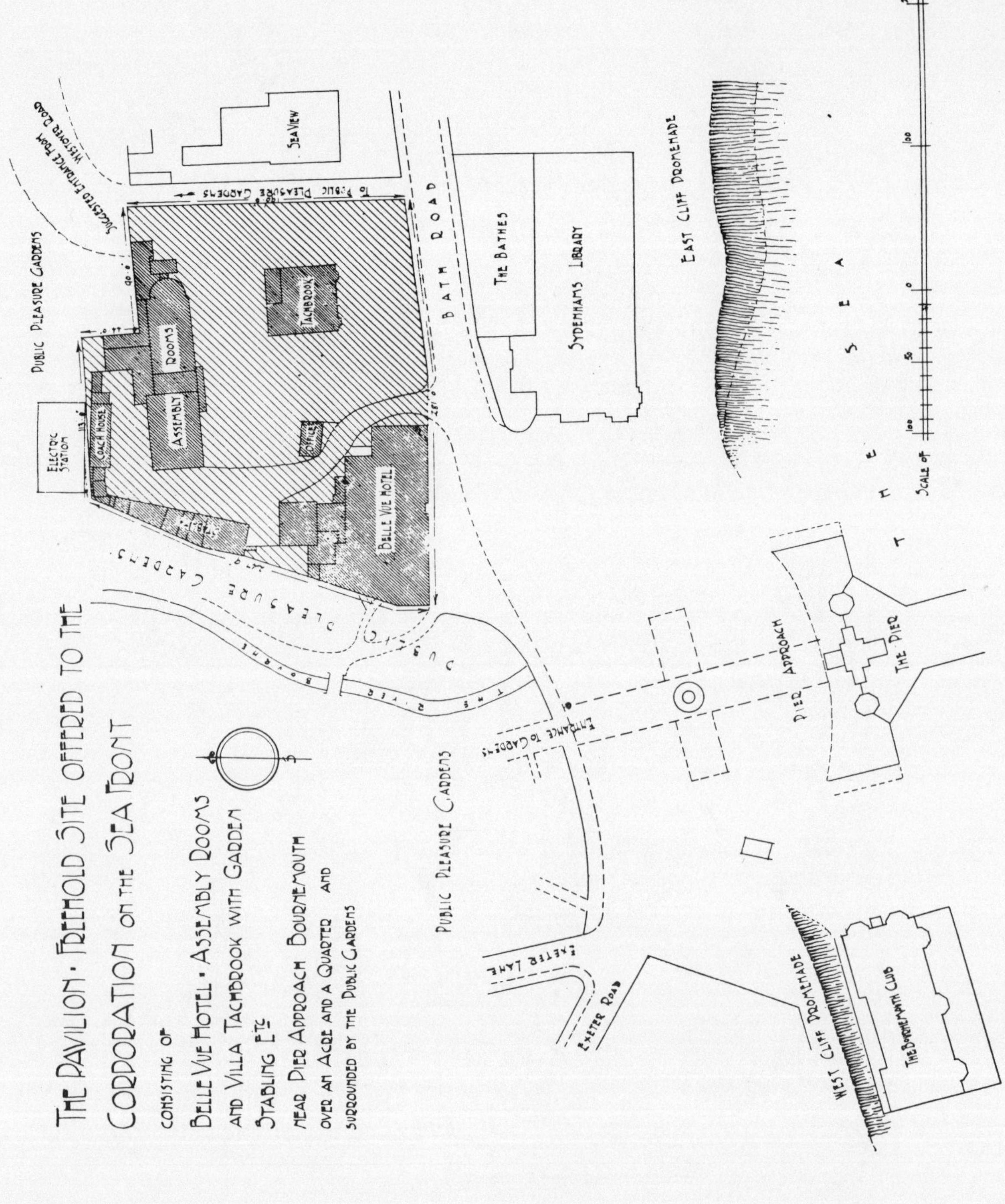

A plan in the *Bournemouth Graphic* of 1 February 1906 shows the site intended for a pavilion. (DCL)

A Most Agreeable Promenade

'Started for Bournemouth a Sea place between Christchurch and Poole', wrote Lady Heathcote in her diary for 3 July 1843. A month later she returned home to Hursley, noting 'the shore from lack of Fishing or Pleasure boats uninteresting, and except on foot, difficult to reach the way to the shore being very heavy and deep in loose sand, the air is fine and bracing'.

Most resorts had a street of hotels and shops behind the beach, and a promenade on a sea wall would protect the cliffs. A local company's scheme in 1882 was for 'esplanade, acquarium, boating club-houses, museum and établissement' from pier to Durley Chine. Prompted by Southbourne's attempt in 1885, the Commissioners offered prizes for a design, and the Town Council rejected its Borough Engineer's scheme in 1893.

Archibald Beckett's plan, supported by Sir George Meyrick, for a drive with shops from the Highcliff Hotel to Boscombe pier, provoked the Council to approve its own scheme in 1897. A 'Flying Squadron' was sent to inspect such attractively-named Continental resorts as Middelkerke and Blankenberghe, as well as the English coast from Dovercourt to Scarborough. In November 1907 the first length, from the pier to Meyrick Road, was opened, and extended to Boscombe. When Lady Meyrick was asked to open the East Cliff lift in 1908, Sir George hoped they would not have to travel on the cliff railway.

A shelter for donkeys was to be adapted for an office in 1985, though they had not been used for years. Grantley Berkeley in 1865 described 'innumerable donkey-chairs labouring through heavy sands' and their impatient drivers. 'The loud and continuous drumming of these boys with their sticks on the donkey's ribs ought to be melancholy music to the patient who occupies the little four-wheeled chair.'

In 1928 the promenade was extended to Alum Chine, in 1950 east to Marine Road, and in 1957 west to the county border. Between the two piers in the 1930s was a drive for cars, which crawled along at eight miles an hour and parked in black lines in front of the beach huts. Small 'toastrack' 'buses gave a summer service. In the 1950s, pressure of increasing motor traffic closed the through road in summer; later, a pier pedestrian precinct formed by the flyover blocked the drive from the west.

Though some cliff falls still occur, seventy years of sea wall has reduced the width of beach. Captain Denham in his survey for a jetty in 1847 remarked that 'the sea does not recede more than one hundred yards from the line of bold cliffs'. For several months in 1977, sand was dredged from the bay and pumped ashore, but high water still washes the base of the sea wall.

The Town Council's new broom of 1890 swept the sand clean, refusing licences for such excesses as swing boats, shell fish stalls, a coconut stand, comedians and ice cream. More sober entertainments of air balls, a bird stand, and microscope exhibitor were considered suitable. Early this century several concert parties performed in 'pavilions' on the beach — Birchmore and Lyndon's 'Gay Cadets' and Willie Cave's 'Revels'. In 1922 the Council's auction of thirty annual beach licences for the season included a punch and judy show, and £10 for a weighing machine site that still exists east of the pier.

'The beach', announced Sydenham's *Guide* in 1840, 'easy of access, forms a delightful promenade at any state of the tide, being of a fine, firm sand'. This is just as true today, though there is less of it. And if, in viewing the 'miles of golden sand' the town advertises, the visitor includes the western reaches belonging to Poole, no harm is done.

A caricature of 1816 showing seaside activities of the Tregonwell and Grosvenor families does not show them near the water, but in 1824 Mrs Arbuthnot wrote in her *Journal* of 'a gentleman of the name of Tregunwell, who has built four or five beautiful cottages which he lets to persons who go for sea-bathing. I was so charmed with the beauty of the situation that Mr A. and I have half decided to take one next summer for the sake of a little bathing'. She does not record the other half of the decision.

'Two modern detached houses to let' advertised the *Salisbury and Winchster Journal* in 1826; 'a bathing machine and a warm bath'. Sydenham in 1840 mentioned 'the machines . . . well attended, being very convenient and always available'. He was tenant of the Belle Vue when the owner Samuel Bayley had to auction his property, including lease of 'a strip of land . . . on the West side of the river Bourne . . . measuring about 300 feet in length, with the exclusive right of Bathing and of Standing Machines for Bathing on the Beach, for half a mile on each side of the river, together with three buildings under the cliff in front of the Bourne Baths', as well as four bathing machines and shares in the Bournemouth Bathing Company.

Borough by-laws of 1897 forbade users of the foreshore to 'beat or shake any carpet, drugget, mat, rug or fabric . . . shout or brawl or sing, or utter any song or ballad . . . ring any bell, or sound any gong or blow any horn or trumpet . . .'. But the pier landing stage was free to bathers from five to eight each morning. The Council offered for tender 'old single and double bathing machines' at Durley Chine in 1928.

Sydenham in 1840 advertised his 'suite of commodious warm baths, combining every desirable accessory . . . erected immediately contiguous to the beach'. They were extended in 1864, so that Brannon's 1880 *Guide* was able to describe them as 'well arranged and convenient. The building itself, adjoining the Library, is fitted up with every accommodation for hot, cold and vapour baths'. A swimming pool was added in 1887, and Sydenham's Baths lasted half a century more.

The souvenir brochure of the new baths (opened on 25 March 1937) gives the cost, with sun-bathers' terrace and solarium, as almost £70,000. It closed at the end of the summer Aquacircus season in 1984; the site whose freehold Sir George Meyrick had sold sixty years before for £6,000, is valued at £1¼ million.

The prophetic Dr Granville on his visit in 1841 had recommended that 'a short pier . . . convenient for landing on the beach in favourable weather, ought to be added'. Captain Denham, Marine Surveyor, visited Bournemouth in 1847 and, praising its natural features, recommended that 'the only adjunct requisite to render this combination of properties perfect is a Jetty . . . Although the Steam Packet between Poole and Portsmouth passes within two miles of that part of the Bay, and the yachts of the Isle of Wight Waters frequently cruise in the Bay and stand in, yet no intercourse can be calculated for want of a Landing Jetty'.

To give four-feet draught at low water, suitable for open boats, Captain Denham estimated that a 250-yard structure would cost £1,642; extension to 450 yards for steamers and yachts would add £834. A cross-jetty and waiting rooms would take the complete cost to nearly £4,000. 'The Timber Pile Jetty or Pier . . . shall answer all the required accommodation for Passengers and Equipage, will facilitate Water Excursions, and present a most agreeable Promenade' — but none was then built.

By 1855 Brannon's *Guide* noted 'the new landing jetty . . . close by the brook . . . a tramway on piles, so that the top or platform can be drawn off at any time'. It was only six feet wide and a hundred long. Four years later, with the Commissioners now in charge, the engineer John Rennie, famous for harbour works and knighted for his rebuilding of Waterloo Bridge, was asked for a design. That was on 1 March; by late July the first piles were driven, and in 1861 Bournemouth's first pier was opened by Sir George Meyrick. The toll was a penny, but residents' season tickets were available, costing five shillings to a guinea according to the rateable value of the holder's property. This paid the toll-collector 12s a week, though he was allowed two suits and hats yearly.

By 1886 some wooden piles had to be replaced by cast iron, as a result of 'the worm', and the next year the pier lost not only its new toll-house but 300 feet of its length. The Promenade Pier Company's proposal for a new structure costing £17,000 was withdrawn. Meanwhile another 100 feet of length was demolished, and a temporary landing stage was built for steamboats in 1877. That year a London periodical described 'the rickety old ramshackle pier . . . a positive disgrace to cheerful Bournemouth'.

Only three years later, in 1880, a new pier was opened by Sir Francis Truscott, Lord Mayor of London. It had cost £23,000 and was 838 feet long — extended to 1,000 feet in 1894. Along its echoing boards many thousands of visitors strolled, (or hurried) to the steamers; they sat in the glazed shelters along its sides, and listened to the twopenny band concerts. Its spiky turreted entrance was replaced by plainer contours in 1929. Piermasters were men of authority and prestige; appointed in 1934 was Captain A. J. Moss, who had been Senior First Officer on the *Aquitania*. The era ended suddenly in 1940, when in July the Royal Engineers blew a breach in the pier to prevent its use for enemy landings, and throughout the war it was a symbol of broken peace. When the gap was bridged on 29 April 1947, it seemed that a link was forged again with pre-war days, though the decking was not open till November, and it was 1950 before reconstruction of the pier-head began. Ten years later its theatre was opened. Meanwhile many piers in Britain had been wrecked or merely abandoned as unsafe and uneconomic. The Council took an enterprising view, and began urgent reconstruction in 1979. On 16 July 1981 came the official opening of the Pier and Leisure Centre.

It was Florence Newlyn in 1878 who pronounced the first stone laid of the new Bournemouth pier, adding: 'And I shall remember it as long as I live'. She was eight. Lady Shelley drove the first pile of Boscombe pier ten years later. Locally designed and built, it belonged to a private company until the Council bought it in 1904, enlarging it in 1926-27. Boscombe pier too was breached in July 1940 as an anti-invasion measure. For many years it had not been used as a landing-stage, and reconstruction did not start till 1958. The pier head was given a roller-skating rink, replaced in 1965 by an amusement centre. As a poor relation of Bournemouth pier, it has at least survived.

In 1914 the first *Skylark* began trips round the bay. Between the wars the fleet was built at Poole, including the *Titlark* in 1936. They used a wooden jetty on cartwheels just east of the Pier. When Jake Bolson died in 1953, aged 64, he had worked nearly all his life on Bournemouth beach as a boat proprietor; he left Bolson's jetty in many memories.

In 1830 the *Independent* coach called at the George and Dragon in Christchurch every weekday at noon on its way to Poole. Twelve years later it was the *Emerald* coach from the King's Arms where on weekday mornings at 8.30 the coach for Salisbury was the *Bournemouth*. Proprietor of the King's Arms was Henry Newlyn, who in 1870 extended his buisness to the Exeter Hotel. In 1842 there was also a carrier, James Sparks — 'from his house, Poole road, every Tuesday, Thursday and Saturday'. The track westwards was still the Poole road, in which Bournemouth was only an incident.

ABOVE: The pier on a summer evening at the turn of the century. Opened in 1880, it was rebuilt a century later. BELOW: The first pier of 1861, used by steamers until 1877 and rebuilt in 1880. (Both DCL)

ABOVE: Boscombe pier, opened in 1889, was used by paddle steamers in its early years. The skeleton of a 65-foot whale, washed up in 1897, was erected on the pier, and is visible in front of the twin-funnel steamer. (DCL) BELOW: Bournemouth Pier changed little for sixty years, until partial demolition for coastal defence in 1940. Turnstiles gave access to landing-stages below. (DCL)

ABOVE: East Beach from the pier, before the Undercliff Drive of 1907, with refreshment rooms, stalls and bathing machines. LEFT: In the winter of 1908-09 the Council spent £300 on making the East CLiff Zig-zag out of Steps Chine, also known as Meyrick Steps. RIGHT: Advertisement in Mate's *Bournemouth Illustrated* in 1886. (All DCL)

ABOVE: East Undercliff Drive on a sunny morning in the early 1920s.
BELOW: East Beach from the pier, whose ironwork and 14 glazed shelters lasted to 1940. (Both DCL)

ABOVE: Bank Holiday fair on the East Beach in 1890. BELOW: A mid-19th century view, with St Peter's spire sketched in. (Both DCL)

ABOVE: The formal opening of the pier by Sir Francis Truscott, Lord Mayor of London, on 11 April 1880. CENTRE: Paddle-steamers used the pier from 1868 and (except for war years) until 1966. BELOW: John Newman's engraving, published by the New Marine Library shows the pier of 1880. (All DCL)

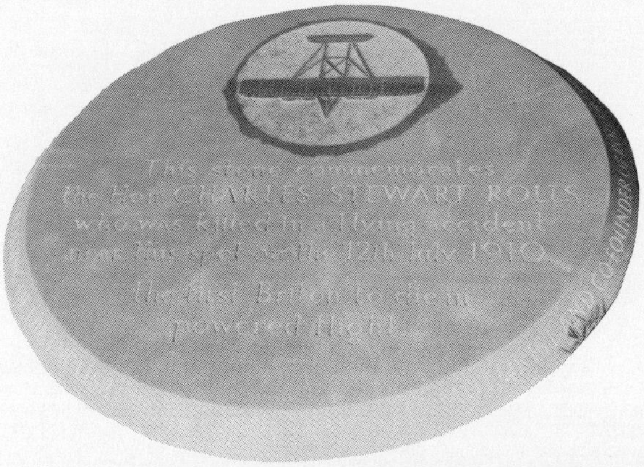

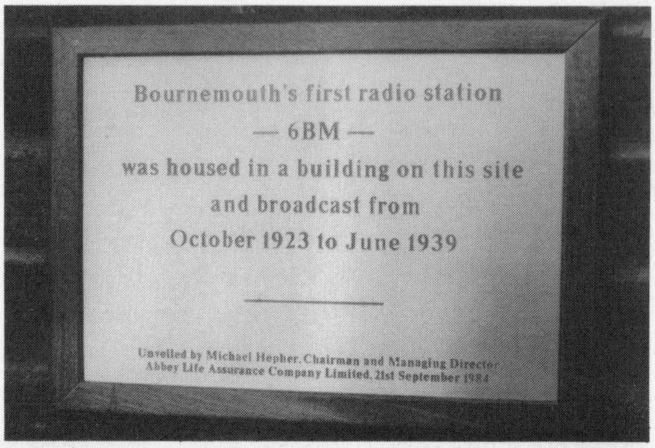

LEFT: A memorial tablet to C. S. Rolls was placed in 1978 near the site of his fatal flying accident in 1910. RIGHT: Plaque on Abbey Life offices in Holdenhurst Road. (Both A) BELOW: Five trams wait in the Square, the nearest bound for Ashley Road. The shelter existed from 1925 to 1949. (DCL)

Train to Airport

The railway linking Southampton and Dorchester in 1847 carefully avoided Bournemouth. Named 'Castleman's Corkscrew' after its promoter, it passed through Wimborne and reached Hamworthy; from Christchurch Road Station (later renamed Holmsley) passengers could undertake the twelve-mile journey by horse drawn 'bus, that ran three times daily to the Bath Hotel.

Plans for a rail route to Holdenhurst from West Moors were opposed by the Earl of Malmesbury and Dr Farr of Iford House. The line to Christchurch from Ringwood in 1862 was planned with low engineering costs, so the speed limit of 25 mph was in places reduced to 15. Fares were a penny a mile third-class, and 1½d for a calf or pig. An omnibus took passengers on to Bournemouth for 1s 6d.

The *Bournemouth Visitors' Directory* complained of almost six hours to London on wooden seats, and the dear second-class fare of 28s — 'a cause of paucity of summer visitors to the place'. To be profitable, the line had to reach Bournemouth, though the Commissioners insisted it should end 'out in the brickfields'. It was opened in 1870, terminating on the east side of Holdenhurst Road, where, (assured Hankinson's *Guide*), 'every attention and civility is devoted to strangers and visitors'. Not mentioning the attitude to residents, the *Guide* complained that to London was still 'a half-day's journey . . . This evil will, it is hoped, in time be remedied'.

Russell-Cotes recalled that, when first he asked for a ticket to Bournemouth, the booking-clerk at Waterloo had not heard of it. In 1888 a direct line from Brockenhurst, long opposed by the New Forest authorities, was opened. Always cautious, the *Bournemouth Observer* remarked that 'the Ringwood Line is preferable in respect of . . . landscape beauty'. The track now passed under Holdenhurst Road to a new station costing £50,000. It was still called Bournemouth East until 1899, because the LSWR had plans for a new Central station only 200 feet from Branksome Wood Road, 'designed with due regard to architectural effect, and have the appearance rather of a winter garden than a railway station'. The site would have been near Braidley Road.

The Dorset Central Railway also planned a station near the Square, but their line from Bath, completed in 1874, reached only just within the Commissioners' one-mile radius. It gave direct access from the Midlands, so that 'one day we are crowded with miners, the next with shoemakers'. When, in the first summer, the LSWR proposed Sunday excursion trains, the Commissioners objected that they 'would necessitate the opening of public houses and refreshment rooms . . . interfere with the quietness of the Sabbath . . . not at all conducive to the best interests of the town'. They had wanted the route joining East and West stations to pass north of the cemetery, and managed to have nearly all the LSWR line concealed in cuttings. A steam excavator spent the summer of 1884 in Talbot Woods. Between Iford and Branksome it passes over only one road — at Meyrick Park. It was remarked that one could spend some time in the town without noticing a railway at all.

There might have been more. Early plans included lines from Poole and Wimborne direct to Christchurch and, in 1845, for a Bristol, Poole and Lymington railway. Several schemes involved Christchurch Harbour; in 1884 it was proposed to narrow it to 500 feet with a dock. Bournemouth Pier was suggested in 1874 for a rail and steamboat link to Swanage.

The LSWR, it has been said, 'dragged the town kicking and screaming into the 19th century'. The first London train in 1888 had taken three hours; by 1900 a train before nine could take daily commuters. Stations opened at Pokesdown in 1886 and Boscombe in 1897; for Winton a halt by Meyrick Park bridge existed from 1906 to 1917. On weekdays in 1910 forty-one trains left the Central, and twenty-nine from the West for destinations through Poole. A through service to Brighton began in 1908.

In the 1920s there were 6s 6d day returns to Waterloo. The *Bournemouth Belle* ran from 1931 in summer, and from 1936 daily. The train that in 1911 had run from Manchester in just over six hours was in 1927 named the *Pines Express,* racing through the Mendips and the Blackmore Vale for scent of the sea. A generation of travellers left the West station on a cross-country route to Midlands and North.

On 28 September 1935 the last train ran on the line through Hurn to Ringwood — a hint of closures to come. In 1964 the service to Salisbury and on the 'old road' through Wimborne and Ringwood ended; next year Bournemouth West and Boscombe stations closed. Affection for the old Somerset and Dorset line could not save it in 1966, and next year Bournemouth saw its last steam train. Electric services now reach London in a hundred minutes.

Paddle-steamers and Bournemouth were together for almost a century. They awaited a landing-stage, but in 1868 Sydenham charted the *Fawn*, of Southampton, for the Spithead Review. His next two steamers lost money, but he was appointed manager for George Burt of Swanage, who bought the first, used regularly at Bournemouth. The *Heather Belle* served six summers from 1871, and the Bournemouth Promenade Band played for passengers. The *Criterion* in 1877 offered a £1 excursion to Cherbourg, though the Commissioners raised pier tolls to discourage Sunday excursions.

The next few years into the 1880s saw competition; one company offered a return trip with the Royal Italian Band to the Isle of Wight for 4½d. The new pier of 1880 allowed four vessels to berth. Owners of the *Lord Elgin* assured the public of 'strict instructions to the captain on no account whatever to attempt racing'. She averaged 13 knots, but used too much coal and was withdrawn. In 1881 the *Empress* visited Brighton, while other destinations were Torquay, Dartmouth and Alderney.

Many were the nostalgic names — *Monarch* (on Bournemouth service from 1888 to 1950), *Majestic, Consul, Emperor of India.* The *Empress* and *Victoria* possessed strengthened bows for beaching at Lulworth Cove. The *Bournemouth* was the only steamer wrecked, running aground at Portland in fog in 1886, and scrapped for £7 10s. The *Windsor Castle*, found too unstable and extravagant for Bournemouth, was sold to the Scots.

All services ceased on 2 September 1939, and some steamers on war service were worn out or lost. On 19 August 1946 the *Princess Elizabeth* arrived from Southampton, joined next month by *Embassy* and *Monarch*; it seemed the old times were back. But people were tired of the same routes, and soon preferred to be motorists; higher safety standards were imposed on ageing ships. The *Monarch* was withdrawn in 1950 when the fare to Swanage was 7s 6d though, in the next season, three steamers still used the pier. But by 1964 the *Embassy* was the only paddle-steamer at Bournemouth, and after the 1966 season was seen no more.

Anyone who remembers the paddle steamers can imagine again the sound and smell of a summer's day at the pier. They were sighted rounding the point from Swanage, identified by their shape, recognised by name. Bailey the photographer blew a whistle to attract attention from the deck. The last trip of the day was to berth at Poole — the cheapest voyage of all —

as sun set over the Purbecks and harbour buoys flickered. It was hard to leave the deck for the oily warmth of the engines — always on view to passengers — where shining rods slid, the paddle-wheels beat and splashed in their boxes. The green 'bus back to Bournemouth was another world.

'They do not run in accordance with the published timetables', reported the Hackney Carriage Inspector in 1897, observing the town's 97 licensed omnibuses. His 1913 report to the Horse Committee listed 444 drivers including 77 of 'Bath Chairs drawn by pony, ass or goat, or propelled by hand'. No goats are remembered, but hire of a donkey or hand chair cost a shilling the first quarter-hour, then sixpence each thirty minutes. One driver would have been W. J. Butt, who in 1943 had been bath chair man 49 years, and was the last.

By 1913 there were seven motor 'buses and 36 licensed porters with handcarts. The town had 46 carriage stands besides those at the stations, and one of the 23 cabmen's shelters remains at the corner of Iddesleigh Road. Almost 500 cabs were registered by 1927 in a total of 8,000 motor vehicles. Outside Beales, black limousines waited, each with its uniformed chauffeur.

The first horse 'bus enterprise was in 1866, when Francis Graham operated a service between the West station and town centre, and later to the East station when it opened. He was a Scot who had settled near Holdenhurst. His sons operated from West Cliff Mews in St Michael's Road and later used premises now the Savoy garage.

When trams began in 1902, horse 'buses could not compete on the new routes and turned to operating tours. Graham took the Kaiser in 1907 from Highcliffe Castle on a tour to Devon and Cornwall. The town guide for 1912 advertises Mark Briant of South Cliff Mews in Exeter Road as 'Taxi-Cab Proprietor and Jobmaster — High Class touring cars — from 9d a mile'. In the same year 'A. W. Futcher's Express Coaches and Charabancs leave the Square for the New Forest, Wimborne and Canford Model Village'.

Charabancs were given even numbers only, to exaggerate the size of the fleet, when Bournemouth and District Motor Services formed in 1916. In July 1919 the firm began a route from the Square to Ringwood. A Poole, Blandford and Wimborne service began in 1920, extended two years later to Shaftesbury. After a Wallisdown firm was bought in 1924, twenty-six 'buses daily ran there from the tram route at Winton, and four penetrated to East Howe. From the same year dates the familiar name of Hants and Dorset Motor Services.

Surfacing of New Road to the river bridge in 1928 brought new routes to Ferndown, while competition with smaller firms reduced fares — Wimborne return by 1930 was 6d. Hants and Dorset's chance came when Poole agreed to its 'buses replacing Bournemouth's trams as far as Westbourne, and from the first day of 1929 the 'green buses' ran to the Square — 5d from Poole. On 9 March 1931 its palatial white 'bus station, stated to cost £1 million, opened on the corner of Exeter Road facing the Square.

The building was shared with Royal Blue coaches, which had their origin in Thomas Elliott's service to Holmsley station. About 1880 Elliott had the Royal Blue and Branksome Mews in Avenue Lane, (now Marks and Spencer's site), operating soon to Westbourne, Boscombe and Winton. In 1911 the firm began motor taxis, and from 1913 its new charabancs were called motor coaches. Tour were expensive in relation to incomes; a Blandford run cost 5s.

From 1931 the single-deck Royal Blue coaches dived into the station basement; Hants and Dorset mounted a ramp to duck below the roof. The 'green buses' became accepted invaders of the Square; an hourly red one was a Wilts and Dorset for Salisbury. In the 1970s they became National and red, and since 1983 the name of Wilts and Dorset has been revived for all of them. Bournemouth's own 'buses have become 'The Yellows', advertised in a series of catching slogans. The 40% of Bournemouth households without cars is either the reason for, or a result of, the success of Bournemouth Transport.

Horse-drawn omnibuses were run by several companies from 1889. Trams began in 1901 in Poole, but ran only as far as County Gates, since Bournemouth was concerned at their noise and speed. When in 1902 they first wound from the Lansdowne to the top of Poole Hill, power was taken from a conduit between the rails to avoid poles and wires.

Four years later the system was complete, with depôt and generating station adjoining the railway in Southcote Road, tram sheds at Moordown and Pokesdown, and Rush Corner renamed Cemetery Junction. On 17 October 1905 the Mayor's tram, No 1, decorated with flags outside, red carpet and cane-back chairs inside, led a procession over Tuckton Bridge to Christchurch and back, stopping at both places for speeches, with a Winter Gardens tea at Bournemouth.

It was in Bournemouth that Britain's worst tram accident occurred on May Day 1908, when brake failure on the descent through Avenue Road caused No 73 to overturn into the garden of Fairlight Glen — a private house which later became the transport lost property office. Seven were killed, and an enterprising publisher made picture-postcards of the scene to interest one's friends.

All trams except the Mayor's (which could be chartered for special occasions) were double-deckers, but the Board of Trade would not allow covered tops, because the tracks were a narrow gauge 3′ 6″. Bournemouth people still recall the brown wooden seats which could be turned over to a dry side. No Sunday trams ran until 1913 when services started at 2pm, extended to mornings in 1926.

The Council was able to boast in 1910 a system of over 29 miles of track, which had carried almost 14 million passengers in their 81 cars. A timetable for August 1914 shows the first weekday journey leaving Poole for Christchurch at 5.14am, and the last at 9.52pm. On the 'main line' of eleven miles, the journey took almost ninety minutes at an average speed of seven miles per hour — but it cost only 9d. By 1928, after 25 years, the trams were still earning money for rate relief, though the new motor 'buses lost £3,000 in the year. A motor 'tram-o-car' service ran along the Undercliff Drive to Boscombe Arcade.

The lease on lines beyond County Gates was for only thirty years, and Poole arranged for Hants and Dorset Motor Services to take over the routes in 1929. With Kinson and Wallisdown likely to join Bournemouth, the Council considered the future of public transport. In 1933 four trolleybuses of various colours appeared in the Square for a trial service to Westbourne, and by the end of the year the Council decided to replace trams. On 8 April 1936 the last one ran between Christchurch and the Square amid excitement similar to the first, thirty-one years before. The Mayor's tram became a 'bus shelter at Iford.

If not the largest, Bournemouth's trolleybus system became the most comprehensive in Britain, and it was the only one to have open-top services in summer. By 1951 when the last route was opened, trolleys glided among Castle Lane fields and Talbot Village trees. Their profits contributed to rate relief; new tariffs in 1951 retained a penny fare, though dogs were to travel at children's rates. Next year the Transport Department celebrated sixty years of Bournemouth public transport.

On 20 April 1969, the day after their final services, the last twelve trolleybuses processed to Christchurch and back. Bournemouth now had 'buses just like any other town.

Fields near Vine's Farm at Wallisdown were the scene of Bournemouth's first flying. W. E. McArdle and the American aviator J. A. Drexel in May 1910 organised a display, enlivened by the Winton brass band. McArdle had been Kaiser Wilhelm's guide at Highcliffe Castle in 1907, honoured with the Order of the Red Eagle. Two years later he gave up his engineering business, Motor-Mac's in Holdenhurst Road, to concentrate on flying.

For a fortnight in 1910 Bournemouth celebrated its Centenary with a programme of fêtes, including Britain's first International Aviation Meeting. For a week the Burlington Hotel was

Royal Aero Club headquarters and a rendezvous for famous flyers. On grassland at Southbourne between Belle Vue Road and Hengistbury, a mile of land was laid out with temporary enclosures and grandstands where the public paid from 2s to 20s. They overlooked a course of 3,140 yards round four pylons. Graham-White won the longest-distance flight with 51 circuits but on the second day (12 July) occurred Britain's first fatal flying accident. In the alighting contest C. S. Rolls' plane broke up fifty feet from the ground and he died of concussion. In 1978 a memorial stone was placed in a corner of St Peter's school playing-fields behind houses in Broadway, close to the spot.

Two years later Henri Farman landed his hydroplane at the pier in a *Daily Mail* travelling display. In April 1913 Meyrick Park playing-fields were the site of Gustav Hamel's looping record. At Pokesdown Henri Salmet gave six passenger flights before overshooting to hit a tree. This did not deter Cyril Beale from being flown by Salmet from Four Elms field at Iford Farm to Meyrick Park, dressed as Father Christmas to advertise his store, finishing his journey by horse-drawn coach led by a brass band.

The town then was beyond range of battlefields, but flying schools at Talbot Village and Ensbury Farm took more aircraft over Bournemouth. Commercial flights began at Ensbury in 1919, sharing the field with National Hunt racing in 1925-26, before ending there the next year.

Meanwhile Bournemouth was the scene of the third Schneider Trophy competition on 10 September 1919. A triangular course of twenty nautical miles extended to Swanage and Christchurch, and 'planes had to land twice between the piers. Owing to fog, none completed the course without penalty, but the prize was awarded to the Italian pilot. The Supermarine seaplane giving three-guinea flights round the bay was prophetic of the Spitfires there twenty-one years later.

Sir Alan Cobham in 1930 gave the Council a confidential report on possible sites for a municipal airport. Of twelve he listed, Littledown was nearest to the town, though a main road would be diverted. Others were at Throop, Muscliff and West Parley. Of East Parley he said it was 'capable of being made into a magnificent aerodrome'. He used it for his own Air Circus, and the Hurn station of Fighter Command opened there on 1 August 1941. Most types of military aircraft used Hurn, including those of the USAF. While Poole Harbour in 1939 became a terminal for passenger flying-boats, by 1944 Hurn was Britain's first international airport. Until Heathrow opened it was the base for BOAC, and Bournemouth nights roared with Lancastrians and Tudors on training circuits. The first Comet crews trained there, and it seemed that the town had a sure future in air travel.

But in 1966 the Civil Aviation Authority suddenly cut its operating hours; it was to close at weekends, and all scheduled services had to end. Local reaction was for Dorset and Bournemouth to buy the airport, reopening it on 1 April 1969. Bournemouth-Hurn has been extended, a new terminal building opened, and direct holiday flights developed. Diversions from London's airports bring business to local hotels and coach firms. Few Bournemouth people know that mail is flown nightly between Hurn and Liverpool.

On the individual site at Hurn, Viscount airliners were assembled, Valiant bombers and Varsity trainers produced. The BAC 1-11 maiden flight was there on 20 August 1963, and hundreds of Bournemouth people worked at Hurn until 1984.

As long ago as 1910 Mate and Riddle's book remarked on C. C. Creeke's liking for winding roads, regretting that he had not widened Old Christchurch Road into a 'thoroughfare from East to West of ample proportions'. Ninety years after Creeke's appointment as Surveyor, the Abercrombie Report of 1946 on the town's future proposed relief roads that would bear traffic away from the centre.

By the 1970s motoring forced such changes on the town. A flyover at the Pier separated vehicles from pedestrians and partly relieved Old Christchurch Road. A new 'spur' road over the Stour into Castle Lane gave direct access from Ringwood on the A31, instead of diversions through Boscombe or Winton.

From Littledown to the Dorset border it cut streets, demolished houses, spanned public gardens and opened up new vistas over the town. Critics of the Abercrombie Report had remarked that Bournemouth would have no centre at all. In fact, the Square is less crowded, pedestrian areas freed, and a town shopping centre realised. Wessex Way has also made quiet areas noisy, dividing commerce and social life. Springbourne is sliced between road and railway. In a few minutes motorists can pass through the town to holidays beyond.

ABOVE: Charabancs wait along the Pleasure Gardens wall, with a Royal Blue booking office near the foot of Richmond Hill. This early-1920s shot is taken from Hugh King's store. BELOW: Tram 14 arrives in the Square in front of several horse-drawn omnibuses. (Both DCL)

ABOVE: The Lower Pleasure Gardens had been laid out in their present form by 1873, half a century before this photograph. The central drive was intended for carriage access to the shore. BELOW: Two boys stare at the camera while a young man counts his fare beside the Royal Blue omnibus in this late 19th century view. (Both DCL)

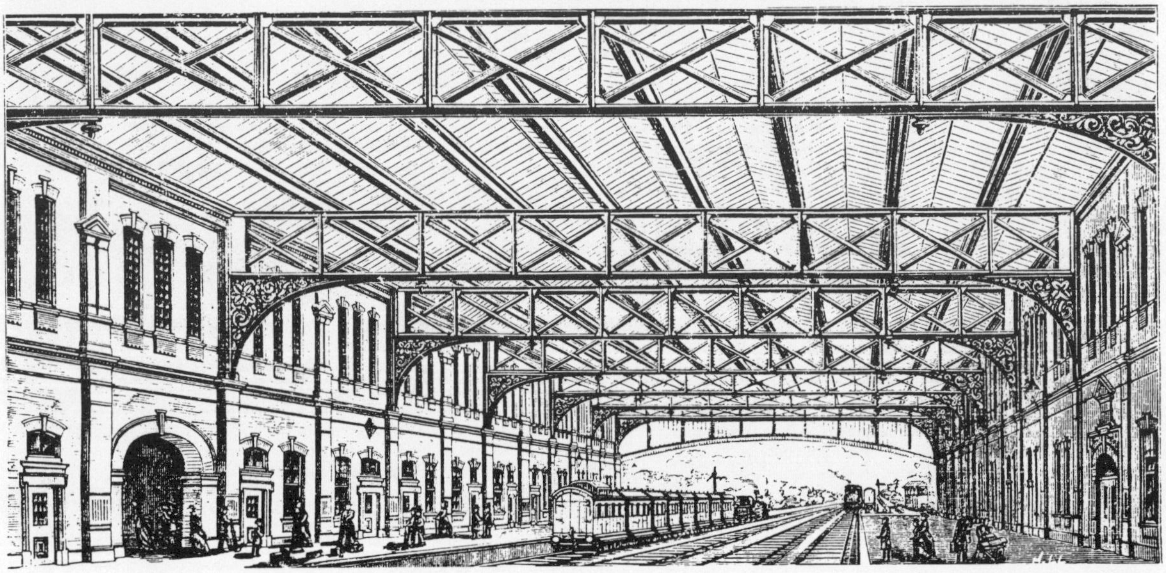

OPPOSITE ABOVE: Hants and Dorset coaches wait in the Square one winter's day about 1930. CENTRE: Bournemouth East Station of 1885 has been the Central since 1899, where a Drummond T9 waits with an up train. The middle tracks were removed at electrification in 1967. BELOW: A year old when illustrated, the new East Station on 20 July 1885 replaced one on the other side of Holdenhurst Road. ABOVE: A steam excavator works on the East station site in the early 1880s, near St Paul's church and the laundry in Littledown Road. LEFT: The Bournemouth, Boscombe and Westbourne Omnibus Company ran this vehicle between Richmond Hill and Winton. RIGHT: *Bournemouth Queen* goes astern from the pier. She was on service from 1908. (All DCL)

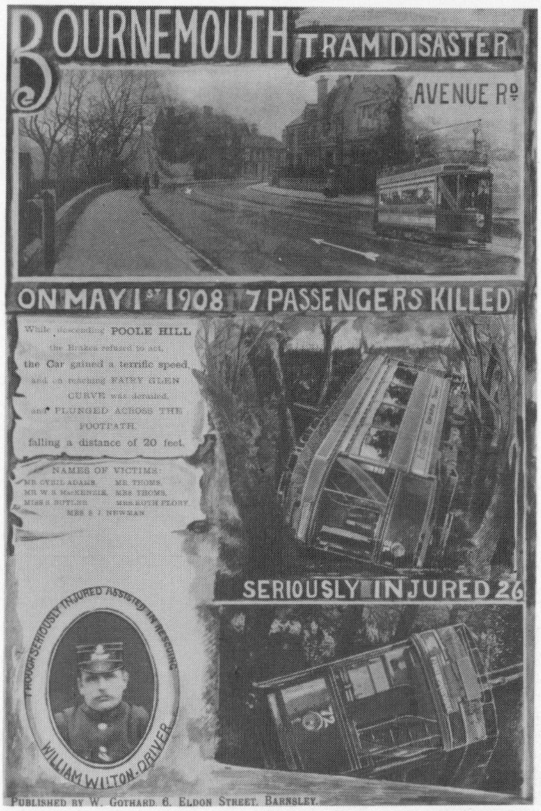
BOURNEMOUTH TRAM DISASTER
AVENUE Rd
ON MAY 1st 1908 7 PASSENGERS KILLED
While descending POOLE HILL
the Brakes refused to act,
the Car gained a terrific speed,
and on reaching FAIRY GLEN
CURVE was derailed,
and PLUNGED ACROSS THE
FOOTPATH,
falling a distance of 20 feet.
NAMES OF VICTIMS:
MR. CYRIL ADAMS
MR. THOMS
MR. W. S. MacKENZIE
MRS. THOMS
MISS S. BUTLER
MRS. RUTH FLORY
MRS. S. J. NEWMAN
SERIOUSLY INJURED 26
THOUGH SERIOUSLY INJURED ASSISTED IN RESCUING
WILLIAM WILTON-DRIVER
PUBLISHED BY W. GOTHARD 6, ELDON STREET, BARNSLEY.

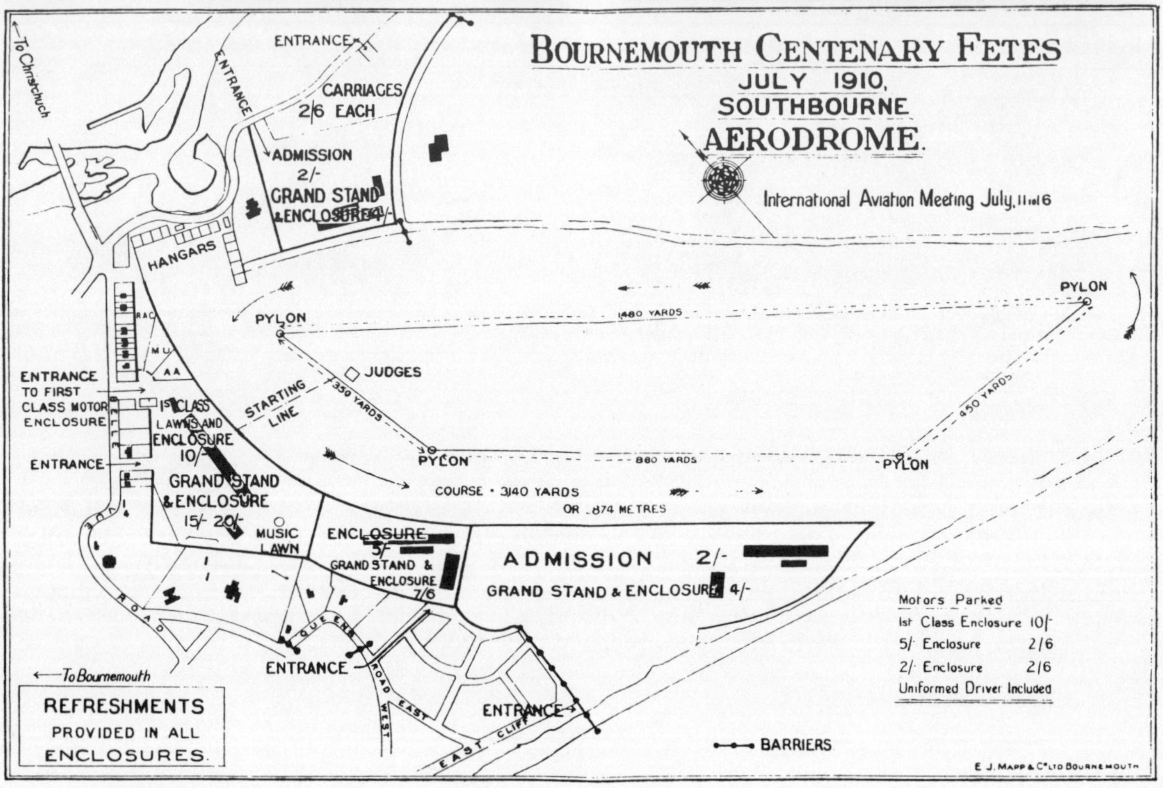
BOURNEMOUTH CENTENARY FETES
JULY 1910,
SOUTHBOURNE
AERODROME.
International Aviation Meeting July, 11 to 16
To Christchurch
ENTRANCE
ENTRANCE
CARRIAGES 2/6 EACH
ADMISSION 2/-
GRAND STAND & ENCLOSURE 4/-
HANGARS
PYLON
1480 YARDS
PYLON
JUDGES
ENTRANCE TO FIRST CLASS MOTOR ENCLOSURE
1st CLASS LAWNS AND ENCLOSURE 10/-
STARTING LINE
350 YARDS
450 YARDS
ENTRANCE
GRAND STAND & ENCLOSURE 15/- 20/-
PYLON
880 YARDS
PYLON
COURSE - 3140 YARDS OR 2874 METRES
MUSIC LAWN
ENCLOSURE 5/-
GRAND STAND & ENCLOSURE 7/6
ADMISSION 2/-
GRAND STAND & ENCLOSURE 4/-
Motors Parked
1st Class Enclosure 10/-
5/- Enclosure 2/6
2/- Enclosure 2/6
Uniformed Driver Included
ROAD
QUEENS ROAD WEST
ROAD EAST
ENTRANCE
To Bournemouth
REFRESHMENTS PROVIDED IN ALL ENCLOSURES.
ENTRANCE
EAST CLIFF
BARRIERS
E. J. MAPP & Co. LTD BOURNEMOUTH

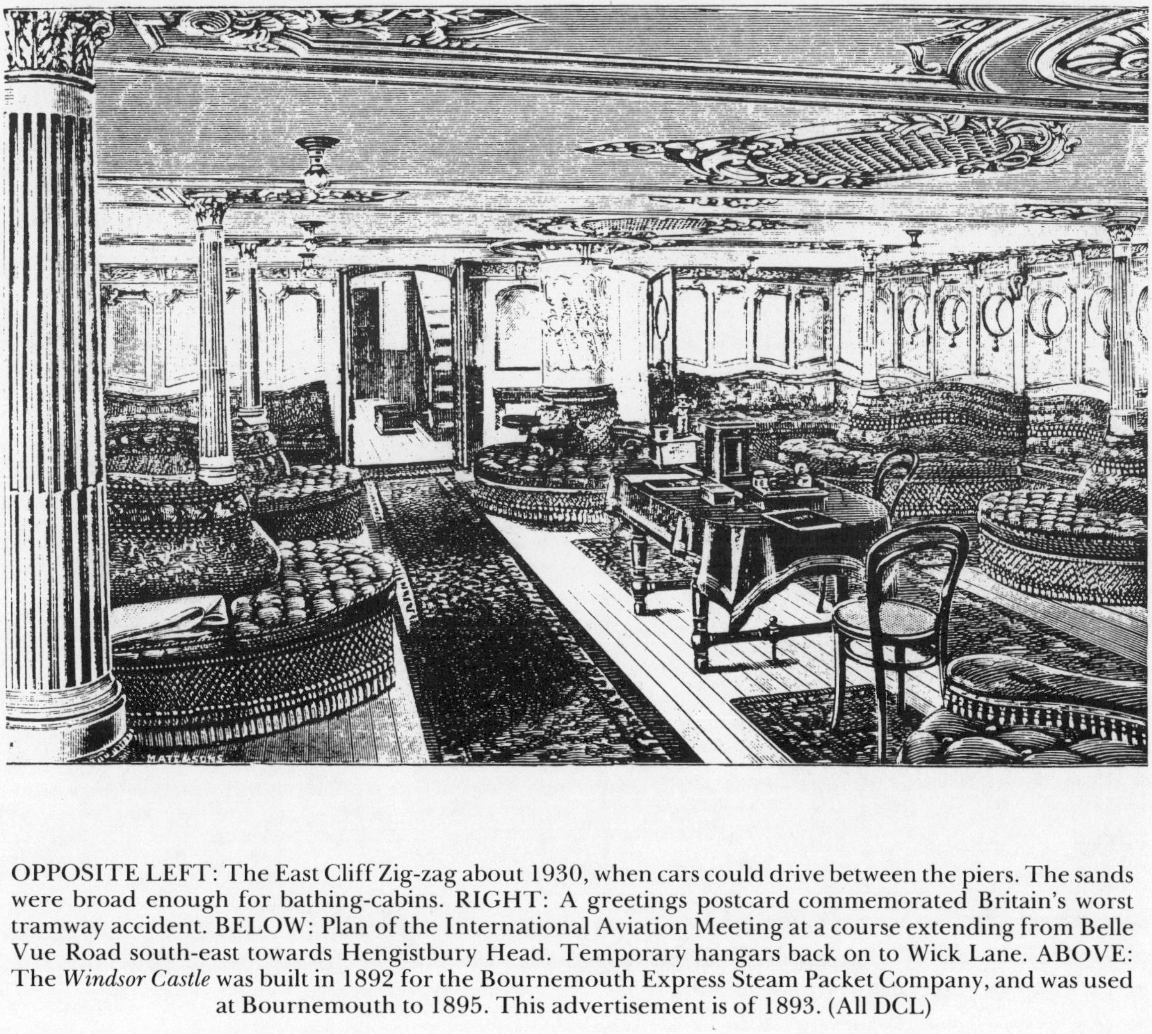

OPPOSITE LEFT: The East Cliff Zig-zag about 1930, when cars could drive between the piers. The sands were broad enough for bathing-cabins. RIGHT: A greetings postcard commemorated Britain's worst tramway accident. BELOW: Plan of the International Aviation Meeting at a course extending from Belle Vue Road south-east towards Hengistbury Head. Temporary hangars back on to Wick Lane. ABOVE: The *Windsor Castle* was built in 1892 for the Bournemouth Express Steam Packet Company, and was used at Bournemouth to 1895. This advertisement is of 1893. (All DCL)

ABOVE: The Municipal College, built 1910-13, was new in this photograph of the Lansdowne. The wing further right is the Lansdowne branch of Dorset County Library. BELOW: Hurn Court is mostly 1830s gothic round a 16th century core. It was the home of Earls of Malmesbury to 1950, and has been an independent school since 1952. (DCL)

A Little Learning

Statistically, Bournemouth has few young people. In the 1981 census the national figure for children under sixteen was 22.3%, for Dorset 19.0%. In Bournemouth only 15.8% of the usually resident population was of statutory school age and below. The newly-born of 1981 are entering schools now.

Bournemouth has the lowest proportion of young people of any county or district in Britain. About one in six is at school, or will be. The other five are responsible (within government limits) for the education and welfare they give the young. From 1903 to 1974 education in Bournemouth was the County Borough's concern through its education committee. With a high proportion of space and wealth, the town would be able to pay for the best in education. Enthusiasm of a few people in the town's history, and now with a County authority, has kept Bournemouth's education alive.

'The profits will be in aid of the funds for Schools and School-houses in Bournemouth', promised Harriet Daniell's book of local lithographs in 1845. 'There is but one school for children of the middle and upper classes, several resident clergyman at present taking pupils', noted Brannon's *Guide* ten years later.

Churches provided the first schools; St Peter's was built in 1850 with an infants' branch in Orchard Street, and had its residential choir school to 1924. The Lansdowne British School began in Commercial Road in 1858, and moved to Madeira Road, adjoining the police station, in 1875. When Holy Trinity founded a school in 1869 it was 'on the outskirts of the town' — later St Paul's. Roman Catholics had started a school in Windsor Cottages, where the Church of the Sacred Heart stands now on Richmond Hill, and its third move in 1880 was to Yelverton Road, where it was called St Walburga's. Since 1928 it has been at Malvern Road, on a site once described as unhealthy. The British School run by the Congregational Church charged no compulsory fees, but the National (Anglican) School at St Peter's required up to 6d a week.

Private education cost much more. At Richmond Terrace, a Collegiate School existed in 1857, as well as two day-schools. Exeter House Collegiate School flourished from 1858 to 1876, when Henry Newlyn bought it for his hotel. Compulsory State education from 1876 encouraged private schools, which increased from a dozen in 1878 to thirty-two in 1886. St Margaret's Hall in West Cliff Gardens was then an Educational Home for Gentlemen's Daughters, and the 1912 *Bournemouth Guide* had ten pages of private school advertisements. Some did not last long, but Cranleigh School in Old Christchurch Road was refounded near the Triangle in 1886 and moved after two years to Norwich Avenue, where it soon extended into several houses, becoming Bournemouth High School for Girls. Land bought for playing-fields in 1926 adjoined a new school in 1935, renamed Talbot Heath. Private high schools with public examination aims were established chiefly for girls, the town's mild climate being considered desirable for them. Boys were sent away to boarding schools, where healthy hardships would fulfil their education.

'Labouring lads of 12 years and upwards' were offered evening classes for 3d a week at St Peter's School in 1864. In higher education a Bournemouth Government School of Art, ('and Science' was an afterthought), began at St Peter's Terrace opposite the school in 1880, but closed by 1891. A similar school on Poole Hill from 1889 was more successful, with evening students; few took science, which more studied at the Pokesdown School of Science, Art and Technical Studies built in 1897. The building is now a clinic.

The Town Council, which in 1895 had declined to take over technical education from Hampshire, found itself in 1903 with an education committee responsible for elementary schools. Of these there were twenty-one — thirteen of them Anglican — and all run by the churches. No School Board had been set up in 1870, since churches claimed they provided adequately. By 1906 the Council had acquired all six nonconformist schools, and several were found in poor condition. The Council's first school was Alma Road in 1908, followed by Winton and Moordown in 1911, and Stourfield in 1912. All fees for elementary education had ended in 1903.

No ancient endowed school existed in so young a town. In 1896 the Council rejected a secondary technical school for boys, though two years later they approved unanimously a pier pavilion costing several times as much. But in 1897 they leased land from the Cooper-Dean estate on East Common in the newly-named Portchester Road, and in 1901 opened Bournemouth Secondary and Technical School. Soon it found a 'grammar' school aim, and in its first three years grew from 54 to 184 pupils. Twelve were boarders, and the minimum age was eight. To encourage parents to commit their sons to education beyond twelve, the Committee offered scholarships — a system that continued to 1944. By 1918 the school had 481 pupils, yet cost the rates £250 a year. The Board of Education commented on such economy as due to high fees, under-staffing and low pay.

Instead of a grammar school for girls, the Committee offered scholarships to private ones. At last a Girls Secondary School opened in 1918, temporarily in the Municipal College and sharing its facilities, while the adjoining Ascham House (once a Private Gentlemen's School) was adapted. Tuition fees were low, no more that three guineas a term — half those of the Collegiate Girls' School — and again the Board commented on low salaries. BSG moved in 1961 to a 17-acre site in Castle Lane.

Generations of students have walked over the date '1910' on the College steps. In fact it took three years more to complete, amid controversy over expense and even its name. The 150-feet clock tower was condemned as extravagance, until a clock presented by the local MP's wife gave it something to support. Meanwhile the four technical schools grew more crowded, in spite of fees the Board thought deterrent. The new building was said to be on the best site in Bournemouth, was well placed for public transport, and in its first year (1913-14) had 780 students.

The College gave vocational courses. In 1909 pressure from neighbours had prevented conversion of Ascham House as a Central School for trade training, which was discussed again in 1924. Figures compiled next year on 621 school-leavers showed that many were in unskilled jobs and 107 were unemployed.

Near new housing areas in Charminster, a Council school (now Summerbee Junior) started in 1928, but Borough extension found more urgent needs in the new area. Hill View School opened in 1932, but temporary accommodation served until both Kinson Council and East Howe Secondary Girls' Schools were built in 1936; a boys' school followed next year.

By then 30% of senior pupils were in secondary schools as recommended by the 1926 Hadow Report. Two more opened in 1940 — Boscombe Senior Mixed in Ashley Road, and Alma Road Senior Girls'. A few weeks later both old and new schools at Alma Road were destroyed in a night air-raid.

By 1919 both grammar schools had long waiting-lists. The Council noted the Board's advice for a new boys' school with more money to run it, and built a wooden hut in the playground. In 1924 it took over Lowther Road hospital as a boys' school annexe. Transfer in 1939 was to a new building in East Way, where pupils had their shoes inspected for nailed soles. Taunton's School, evacuated from Southampton, shared it for most of the war.

In 1945 six senior schools became county secondary, but it was eight more years before a new one opened. That was Summerbee, named after an Education Committee chairman and built on an optimistic scale. It was followed by Glenmoor (1957), the two Oakmeads (1959), eventually Avonbourne (1970) on a 62-acre site, and Portchester (1975). All were in outer parts of the town, while Boscombe Secondary moved out to join Stourfield in 1965 and form a new Beaufort School.

The 1944 Act had proposed a comprehensive system instead of selection for grammar schools. In Bournemouth the idea was consistently rejected, Governors stating in 1965 that 'the present secondary school organisation is fully comprehensive', a change being 'unnecessary and undesirable'. In 1974 the town found itself in a county largely comprehensive, with one of the few selective systems in the country.

Independent schools had helped to fill demand for examination courses. Queensmount was founded as a girls' grammar school and is still at Queens Park. Wentworth at Boscombe combined with another in 1962 and is now Wentworth Milton Mount. St Peter's began as a Roman Catholic school for boys and is still at Southbourne, though the grey-gothic range, formerly the Convent of the Cross, is now a chiropractic college. Others have closed. In Poole Road the Collegiate was run as an independent grammar school, while nearby the private Ringwood Grammar, coming to the town in 1946, lasted to the 1970s.

Many private schools are beyond memory. At St Aloysius College in Poole Road, and later in Surrey Road, the poet Paul Verlaine taught in the 1870s. John Galsworthy was a pupil at Saugheen School in Derby Road. Foxholes and Grassendale Schools were at Southbourne, the Hailey School in Poole Road. Between the wars many were started in private houses at Boscombe and towards Winton.

Few private schools survived war in 1939. Wychwood Preparatory next to Meyrick Park lasted to 1966, and improved state schools competed with the few private ones remaining. For independent schools the countryside was better; one founded in 1952 is at Hurn Court, former home of the Earls of Malmesbury, who had so much to do with the early development of Bournemouth.

Overcrowded by the 1940s, the College had to hire private houses and use the old mansion at Shelley Park. It opened its first extension to the original building in 1957, when the College of Technology was formed. In 1974 it became the Dorset Institute of Higher Education with premises at Weymouth. In 1977 new buildings of the DIHE opened at a Talbot Village site — officially and incorrectly called Wallisdown. Art colleges at Bournemouth and Poole combined in 1963, but only in 1984 left their Lansdowne location for a new one next to the DIHE, where amalgamation looks inevitable.

But it is not a university, though its prospectus states it is 'comparable with polytechnics in its range of courses', having some two thousand full-time students with more on about a hundred part-time courses. Especially apt for the town is its Department of Catering and Hotel Administration. Bournemouth could have been a university town. A quarter of a century ago the Council agreed on a Shelley Park site of 8½ acres, but caution has prevented a University of Bournemouth.

As private schools declined, language schools have grown. Students from the Continent and the Middle East give a foreign flavour to the streets, where strange foods and language fill the air. Bournemouth is designated a Euro-beach.

BB38 (Großblatt 11) Einzelobjekte:

32 Straßenbahn- und Trolleybusdepot der Bournemouth Corporation

33 Autobus- und Trolleybusdepot der Bournemouth Corporation

35 Feldflugplatz

36 Wasserwerk der Stadt Bournemouth

37 Direktion und Autogaragen der Bournemouth Corporation

45 Westover Garage (ca. 500 Personenautos)

46 The Pavilion, Theater

47 Bobby u. Comp. Ltd., großes Warenhaus

48 The Malmesbury u. Pearsons Dairies. Ltd., Großmolkerei

49 Harvey Nichols u. Co., Ltd., Möbelfabrik

50 Gas- und Wasserwerke der Bournemouth Gas und Water Company
mit 2601 t Rohbenzolgewinnung im Jahre 1937.

51 Artillerie-Kaserne mit Lazarett

67 Hants u. Dorset Motor Service Ltd., Autobahnhof und Garage

68 Hants u. Dorset Motor Service Ltd., West Cliff Garage für 130 Personenkraftwagen

69 Hants u. Dorset Motor Service Ltd., Royal Mews Garage für 150 Autobusse

Krankenhaus, Sanatorium
Eisenbahnwerkstätten
Pieranlagen, Landungsstelle
Straßenbahndepots
Garage
Flugplatz
Gaswerk
Tongruben
Ziegelei
Elektrizitätswerk
Wasserwerk, Wasserturm
Wasserreservoire
Kläranlagen
Molkerei
Möbelfabrik

ABOVE: Key to an Ordnance Survey sheet overprinted for the German Luftwaffe in 1941 to show the town's military objectives. BELOW: One of six parachute mines early on 16 November 1940 destroyed Alma Road schools. (Both DCL)

Garrison Town

Bournemouth's foundation was indirectly through a war. Dorset Yeomanry records of 1801 state that Captain Lewis Dymoke Tregonwell was given charge of a coastal division 'from the eastern boundary of the county at a place called Bourne Chine along the north shore to Pool . . .'. The Dorset Rangers' dark green uniform was the first seen at Bournemouth where, in the course of guarding the coast against the French, Captain Tregonwell discovered its attractions.

War and Bournemouth do not seem to go together, yet twice it has been a garrison town. Ample accommodation for billeting and hospitals filled it with uniforms in both world wars. As early as 1866, local men had enrolled in the 4th Hants Artillery Corps, and in 1885 the town became HQ of a 4th Volunteer Battalion — later the 7th Hants Territorials. Their drill hall in Holdenhurst Road opened with a week of Royal Military Sports and Tournament on East Common in May 1896.

The 1910 *Town Guide* had appeared in German as 'Die Fichtenstadt an der See', but no welcome was offered four years later. At outbreak of war, up to 1,300 aliens had to leave the town, and the orchestra was criticised for playing German music. Dan Godfrey recalled that the German Emperor, staying for three weeks at Highcliffe Castle in 1907, had driven through the gardens and along the Undercliff, turning back in fury when he found he could not go on to Boscombe. Two Kinson men had to push his car out of the ford in Millhams Lane. Now a mine exploding on the beach interrupted a Winter Gardens concert.

Several Belgian refugees took the place of musicians who had joined up. On 9 October 1914 soldiers arrived at Boscombe Hospital, and the Mont Dore was taken over for wounded Indians. Over 15,000 troops were billeted in the town, and each Sunday 400 bathed free at the laundry. In December the Territorials left for India, to relieve the Regulars.

From January 1915 no light was to be visible from the sea; photography and sketching were forbidden in public places. Rowing boats were allowed no nearer the enemy than the end of the pier. Patrons of the Westover Palace — 'dainty teas served on the lawn or in delightfully shaded tea lounge' — soon were reading Gallipoli casualty lists in the local press. By the year's end Bournemouth engineering firms were producing shell parts. The Council allowed drilling on Redhill Common, in the parks and North Cemetery. In November the Talbot Village aerodrome was opened by the Bournemouth Aviation Company, which next year bought Ensbury Farm (RFC Winton) for training. Two fatal crashes occurred on Redhill Common in May-June 1918, and next month a fighter fell in Christchurch Road at the Annerley Road corner. Several churches set up 'war shrines' with names of local men serving, and a roll of honour.

Temporary hospitals opened, and nearby in the Upper Gardens a YMCA hut invited wounded soldiers, who were given teas at the Boscombe Cliff bowling greens and East Cliff cloisters. By contrast with 1939-45, civilian life was slow to change. Petrol was rationed in

1916, sugar from the end of next year, and two milk deliveries cut to one. Someone suggested that tram passengers should queue.

By 1918 war efforts were well organised. In March a Business Men's week aimed at paying for a destroyer, and raised over £¼ million — more than enough. In June the Boy Scouts, who were acting as messengers and coast watchers, paraded in Meyrick Park with 2,000 Girl Guides, for inspection by Sir Robert Baden-Powell. There three weeks later 5,000 people attended a Great Intercession Service.

The Mayor proclaimed the Armistice from the Town Hall in Yelverton Road, and at 1pm led a thanksgiving in the Square. Meyrick Park in September 1919 saw a memorial service for the 650 Bournemouth men killed, whose names are in a Book of Remembrance at the Town Hall. Two months later, the first two-minute silence was observed, trams stopping as power was cut off at the depôt. The War Memorial in the Gardens was unveiled in 1922, and next year the town's smallest park opened as a Hampshire Regiment War Memorial — Fampoux Gardens.

3 September 1939 was a Sunday, when prayers for peace were said in the town's churches at the moment war was declared. ARP headquarters had been set up a Shelley Park manor house, and already there were practice blackouts. In the next few months, as rationing arrived, the Popular Restaurant at the Pavilion became the Food Control Office — later moved to the Anglo-Swiss Hotel.

After six months of distant war, the town began to raise its head. The Pier Approach Baths reopened after use for ARP and first-aid training. Boys of Taunton's School, evacuated from Southampton at outbreak of war, were pictured in caps digging up Strouden Farm. The Council cancelled Boscombe Carnival, reduced the Municipal Orchestra to twenty-four, and raised deck-chair hire to 3d, while in May the Mayor welcomed the Labour Party Conference.

After the Dunkirk evacuation, French troops were billeted on local schools, which were closed for several days. British soldiers filled the large houses of Lansdowne Road, and the RCAF occupied the huge blocks of Bath Hill Court flats. Servicemen drilled on the recreation grounds, billeted in the houses nearby, and trained in Meyrick Park, where an assault course was laid out. The Winter Gardens was taken over, and the Theatre Royal became a service club.

Seventeen minutes after midnight on 3 July, the first bomb fell on Bournemouth, destroying one house in Cellars Farm Road, near Hengistbury Head. That day both piers were closed and, within a few days, explosions cut gas to make them useless. 'Bewurnemothe wer ys feyer landyng' Henry VIII's surveyors had reported exactly four centuries before, was strung with barbed wire along the beaches and cliffs, reinforced later by a line of steel scaffolding in the shallows. With an enemy-occupied coast only 67 miles to the south, the army mounted anti-aircraft guns on flat roofs of beach cafés, and along the cliffs. More were set up in the parks, while steel cables stretched between old lamp-posts across Meyrick Park playing-fields to discourage glider landings.

A week after the first bomb, occurred the first fatality — a civilian 'cyclist in Meon Road. On the western edge of the borough on the same day, eleven bombs fell, causing damage only. The town's position made it vulnerable to two kinds of aerial attack; it was on the route for the industrial Midlands, and it could suffer hit-and-run opportunist raids. 'How Huns waged weekend warfare' the Press remarked after a September raid. After a midday raid at Westbourne in 1940, an enemy plane fell at Branksome and 'a short, ugly, broad-chested Nazi airman' was rescued from the sea. The only Allied airman killed over Bournemouth was Pilot-Officer Hight of the NZAF on 15 August 1940.

In long winter nights there could be fourteen hours between the warning soon after dark, and the all-clear before dawn. Of the worst two raids, one occurred on such a night, when at

3.30 on 16 November 1940, six parachute mines killed 53 and damaged 2,321 properties. About midnight on 10-11 April 1941, bombs burnt out the familiar Woolworths in the Square, as well as damaging Richmond Hill Congregational church and destroying four flats in Fern Bank, St Stephen's Road, where one of the eight killed that night was the Bournemouth poet, Cumberland Clark.

In May 1942 a bomb falling only thirty yards from the War Memorial exploded after seventy-two hours, and the public were advised to report any more suspicious holes. Next month the Anglo-Swiss Hotel was damaged as 'Nazi planes sneaked in through haze' (as the Press reported).

Under similar conditions there occurred the war's worst raid, when an estimated 25 planes attacked at one o'clock on Sunday afternoon, 23 May 1943. The Metropole Hotel at the Lansdowne, and Central Hotel on Richmond Hill, were crowded, largely with service men and women, who accounted for many of the 77 dead. But for most Bournemouth people the memorable loss was Beales', rebuilt only twelve years before, which caught fire and was completely destroyed. In St Peter's opposite, water sprayed on the wooden louvres saved the tower, as ammunition at the anti-aircraft post on Beales' roof exploded.

When the day's disasters were counted, ten incident areas were found. The Punshon Memorial Church on Richmond Hill was damaged beyond repair, like West's Cinema in Old Christchurch Road, privately owned and one of the town's oldest. After damage, Bobby's stores in the Square closed for two months. An enemy plane crashed in Grove Road. That was the last air-raid on Central Bournemouth.

Civil Defence accounted chiefly for a rate rise from 7s 11d to 8s 5d in the pound in 1941; by May 1942 the Council had built public shelters for 40,000. The *Echo* described 'Eastertide at Bournemouth — no outdoor music, no road or rail excursions', and showed a police officer on point duty, wearing a respirator for his five minutes' daily practice.

In July 1941 the *Echo* itself raised its price to 1½d. Some civilian life continued normally: an advertiser for a cook-general offered 25s a week, and for a housemaid 20s (no Irish). A double-fronted house in Holdenhurst Avenue could be rented for £75 a year, excluding rates, a 'detached residence' at 28 Stokewood Road for £80, and a cottage at 25 Windham Road for 16s 6d a week. Furnished property in Moordown was available at 35s and 3 guineas, and a bed-sitting room was wanted there for 5s.

In December 1944, after thirteen months without an air-raid, the *Bournemouth Times* was allowed to publish details up to 29 February. In 958 'red alerts', there had been fifty incidents, causing 51 service deaths and 168 civilian. (For comparison, the total for Southampton was 1,838 killed). Forty-six tons of 2,271 bombs had damaged 13,590 properties. A final raid on 24 April 1944 damaged the new Holdenhurst Road site of West's Cinema. On 21 March a Halifax bomber on a delivery flight had crashed near Meadow Court flats at Moordown, killing its crew of eight and two civilians.

By then coastal areas were closed to visitors, as vehicles marshalled under trees in the parks. After D-Day, the town seemed empty except for aircraft overhead. On VE night the Square was crowded, as Mr Bailey the photographer, who had often used his whistle to catch attention from paddle-steamer passengers at the pier, now did the same from the roof of the tramway shelter.

The town emerged sadly from the war, its beaches barred by obstacles, its two piers wrecked, its town centre stores bombed. Large water tanks lay in wait for fires, and along several main roads stretched steel pipes from pumps at the Stour. The Bourne itself had been dammed at the Square and, in the Upper Pleasure Gardens, a muddy pool renewed for a time the Decoy Pond that Tregonwell had seen in another war.

OPPOSITE ABOVE: Beales, a few days after the town's worst air-raid, on 23 May 1943. BELOW: Bomb damage in Holdenhurst Road, opposite Methuen Road. ABOVE: On 23 May 1943 bombs in ten parts of the town killed 77 people, many of them in the Metropole Hotel at the Lansdowne. BELOW: The Old Christchurch Road side of Beales on Sunday 23 May 1943. (All DCL)

LEFT: Bath Hill Court — a Bournemouth acropolis of 1936. RIGHT: San Remo Towers — Boscombe byzantine of 1938. CENTRE: Redevelopment — the site of St Paul's school in 1984, with the church partly dismantled. BELOW: Bournemouth pier was rebuilt in 1979-83 with a leisure complex at its entrance and a theatre at its head. (All A)

Where Wealth Accumulates

When a Boscombe turnip-hoer was offered an acre of land there for a day's pay, and refused it, he showed both the low value of the land and his earnings — which were four shillings. On a Dorset farm he could have expected half that.

In fact the Boscombe turnip-hoer did well to earn four shillings a day, over a pound a week. Rates of pay for Council employees in 1893 appear in a report by its Surveyor, when there was alarm at the 'present high rate of 1s 10d in the £'. The department was blamed for extravagance, and the Borough Surveyor was instructed to list all his employees and their earnings.

Pay varied from 10s a week for a pier cloakroom attendant to £500 a year for the Borough Surveyor — though perhaps he received no tips. One of the thirty-seven road-sweepers aged 75 had worked for the Council for sixteen years — and still earned only 16s. Gardeners, beach inspectors and lamplighters were paid a guinea, as were the twenty-eight carters employed in 'house scavenging'. The department had over two hundred men, and had been loaded with new responsibilities by the enthusiastic Council.

Within the town's wealth was an element of poverty. In 1870 St Peter's Church ran a Children's Clothing and Shoe Club 'for the benefit of the deserving poor'. For two months of early 1886 a relief committee organised a soup kitchen at Gladstone Road in Boscombe, a voluntary fund offering bread at a penny a loaf, and free coal allowance.

The statutory Distress Committee's report for 1905-6 lists the occupations of 505 applicants for relief. They had been put to work gravel-digging at King's Park, building shelters on golf courses, and trenching Strouden Farm for Bournemouth School's new playing-field. At a cost of £390 forty men had worked on 'making up an old cart track, on the outskirts of the Borough, through the Charminster Estate, so that it would be suitable for ordinary vehicular traffic'. With materials supplied, the outside of the Royal Victoria Hospital had been painted for £50. Average hourly wages in the town were 7½d for painters and 8d for carpenters. Garden labourers were plentiful at 3s 8d a day. In 1939 a Council gardener recalled how forty years before he earned 19s for a 52-hour week. The town's tram crews worked 60 hours and an inspector could reach £1 15s. Six new postal staff in 1873 earned 15s a week, with a shilling bonus for delivering mail to Muscliffe. Not until 1885 did Boscombe shopkeepers agree to shut at 4pm on Wednesdays from May to September, but in the town centre there was no early-closing.

In the 1880s the town was hoping to earn Borough status. Its villas and hotels were full of the most respectable people; the *Observer and Chronicle* listed them twice weekly. In November 1884 it reported the scenes on Poole Hill on 5 November, where over 500 people had assembled. Soon lighted tar-barrels were rolled up and down; a police superintendent and two constables were 'pelted with mud, stones and thick sticks', retreating up Tregonwell road to the Victoria Hotel, where the mob broke several windows. A crowd of about a thousand people, (the report estimated) followed a lighted barrel up the hill, and 'the whole street was given up to the rioters'. By midnight most had dispersed, leaving £200-worth of windows smashed in fourteen shops and three public houses — 'a tale of most disorderly scenes in the streets, and of wilful and reckless damage'. A. J. Abbott recalled Boscombe about the same year, when Saturday nights saw riots between local youths and artillerymen from Christchurch baracks. Outside the coffee tavern at the corner of Palmerston Road, there were regular duckings in the water trough.

'Girls are to be seen driving alone in taxi cabs and on the tops of omnibuses' deplored Sir Merton Russell-Cotes in 1921. In the war, women worked in the town's banks, offices and railway stations, (but not on trams); in 1918 five girls were appointed to library staff, but the ladies' reading-room at Boscombe was discontinued.

Bournemouth was insulated from much of the tearing twenties and dull thirties, its work being chiefly the service and retirement industries. A thousand houses were built in a year, and soon were sold. The Borough had more than its golden jubilee to think about in 1940.

In 1982 the town's deaths exactly doubled births, and its elderly population hardly needs statistics to prove. The 30% over retirement age is almost twice the national average, the town attracting many whose capital and pension have unlocked the door of a modest home. But most have seen Bournemouth first in a holiday season, forgetting that an all-seasons resort includes winter. In 1981 over 12% of Bournemouth people lived alone, and comfortable flats are often lonely ones.

Bournemouth is no longer a growing town — at least in population. Housing almost filled the heathland south of Kinson in the 1950s, and population reached its highest census figure in 1961. Compared with that date, the latest census total in 1981 for Bournemouth is 144,805 — a 6.16% decline in twenty years. Apparently ten thousand Bournemouth people had been lost, while Christchurch and Poole have each grown by some 30%.

By 1961 Poole's population had passed Bournemouth's 1931 figure and, with more land available, Poole was set to outgrow Bournemouth. It was still then a Borough contributing to the county rate and by far the largest town in Dorset. If Poole should become a county borough as Bournemouth had in 1900, Dorset would be left without Poole's large contribution to its income and would scarcely have been economic as a mostly rural county. That problem was solved by redrawing county borders in 1974, when Bournemouth and Christchurch were taken into Dorset as Districts.

The 'new territories' of Bournemouth and Christchurch together have under 4% of the county's area, but contained in 1981 over 30% of its population. Almost a quarter of Dorset people live in Bournemouth. Of the 91 county councillors, 25 represent Bournemouth wards, and another 6 Christchurch.

Three towns together in a few miles of coast seem ready for union as a seaside city. In the late 1940s, when Bournemouth submitted a scheme to the Boundary Commission, it again looked like a take-over bid by the largest, which in 1961 still had more people than the other two combined. Since 1974 Poole has much more unbuilt land than Bournemouth; in the year ending March 1983, completed dwellings totalled 740 in Bournemouth, 1,121 in Poole. For the upper Bourne valley 900 houses are planned — in Poole. They would stand on the skyline seen from Cranborne Chase, near Lewis Tregonwell's home two centuries ago.

Bournemouth is now a business town, with Abbey Life headquarters where once the Holdenhurst Road set out over East Common, and the promise of the Chase Manhattan Bank's office at Littledown.

In the 1970s the Council bought Littledown House and 200 acres of farmland stretching down to Castle Lane — the largest undeveloped area in Bournemouth. A plan in 1980 saw a leisure park there, with such features as an animal collection and maritime museum, with a small area for housing. But in 1983 the Council sold 60 acres to a consortium of three firms, who were to build on 43 acres. The price was over £3½m — more than the Council had paid for the whole estate. The Council's need to sell assets to pay for the Bournemouth International Centre has increased pressure for residential use; an option has been for 950 houses at ten to the acre, leaving 27.5 acres as a neighbourhood park. 'Castledean' has been coined as a name for development at Littledown, where the 200-year old mansion of the Cooper-Deans is to be preserved.

1984 was the year of the BIC. Its leisure pool with wave machines reflects the sea beneath its terraces, and conferences will gather in the 4,000-seat Windsor Hall. (The Pavilion's auditorium could hold just over 1,500, while the Winter Gardens was to be closed as a theatre). The BIC's Smugglers Bar is a reminder of local history, and the Tregonwell Hall is part of the Bournemouth International Centre, opposite the town's first building plot.

Since the Bournemouth Centenary in 1910, three-quarters of a century has passed. If there is another International Aviation week in 2010, what shall we see? As our prophet Dr Granville wrote of the town in 1841 — 'But there is besides, a great deal to be done in the place to render it complete'.

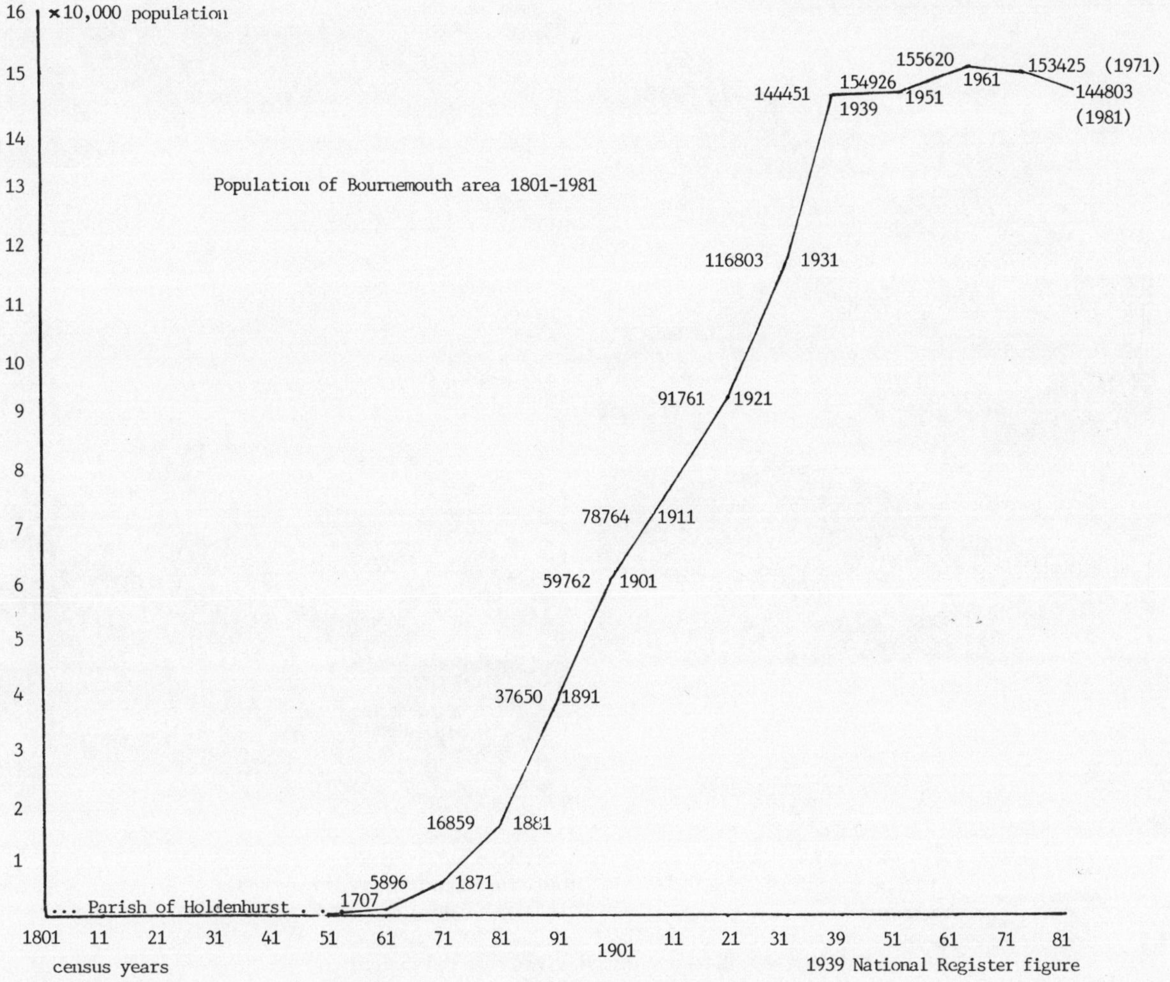

ABOVE LEFT: Richmond Hill in 1984, with St Andrew's tower and part of Debenham's store. RIGHT: Westbourne Arcade was commemorating its centenary when this picture was taken in 1984. BELOW LEFT: The Langtry Manor Hotel in Derby Road, built by the Prince of Wales (later Edward VII) for Lillie Langtry. RIGHT: St Paul's Church tower on 5 January 1985, three days before demolition. (All A)

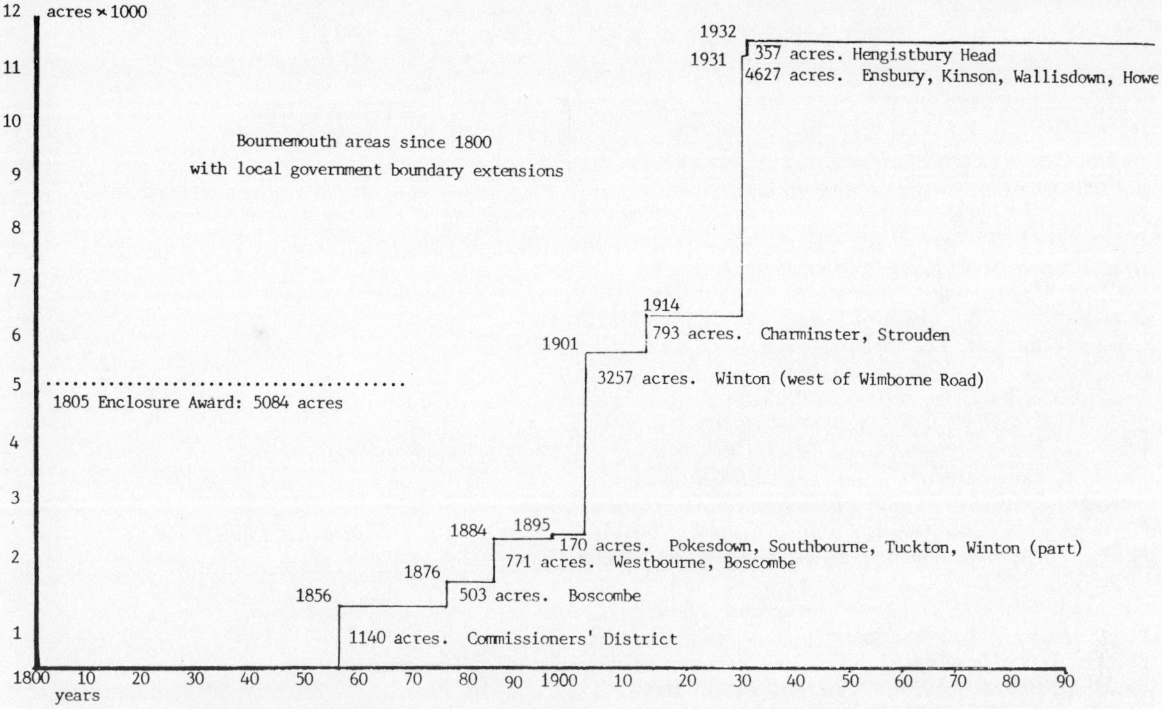

BELOW: The future rises above the skyline: East Beach in January, with flats above the Royal Bath Hotel. (Both A)

Select Bibliography

Anderson, R. D. & G. Frankis. *History of Royal Blue Express Services*. David & Charles. 1970.
Barber, G. *The Bournemouth theatres, 1882 to 1908*. BLSP. 1980.
Barnes, F. W. *Iford: the lost village*. Purbeck Press. 1974.
Bishop, B. *Secondary education in Bournemouth from 1902 to present day*. Bourne Press. 1967.
Brannon, P. *The illustrated historical and picturesque guide to Poole and Bournemouth . . . 1855 and 1880*.
Bray, W. M. *Westbourne: a personal view*. BLSP. 1983.
Bright's *Illustrated guide to Bournemouth*. 1886.
Chilver, K. M. *Holdenhurst: mother of Bournemouth*. 1956.
Cooksey, A. J. A. *Local radio in the Dorset area*. BLSP. 1974.
Cooksey, A. J. A. *The telephone in Dorset*. BLSP. 1974.
Cooksey, A. J. A. *Wireless telegraphy in Dorset*. BLSP. 1975.
Cox, B. *Paddling across the bay*. Paddle Steamer Preservation Society. 1981.
Dale, R. *Reminiscences of Stourfield*. 1876.
Dawson, L. *Wings over Dorset*. Dorset Publishing Co. 1983.
Ford, R. *The history of the Bournemouth police*. 1963.
George, E. A. *Music in Bournemouth*. BLSP. 1979.
George, E. A. *Reminiscences of the cinema in Bournemouth, Poole and Christchurch*. BLSP. 1978.
Gillett, M. *Wanderings in Talbot Village*. BLSP. 1981.
Godfrey, Sir Dan. *Memories and music*. 1924.
Granville, Dr A. B. *The spas of England*. 1841.
Hankinson, T. J. *A descriptive guide to Bournemouth*. 1876.
Harris, J., 3rd Earl of Malmesbury. *Memoirs of an ex-Minister*. Longmans. 1884.
King, M. *Beneath your feet*. Purbeck Press. 1974.
Lands, S. J. *The growth of Winton*. BLSP. 1976.
Lands, S. J. *Old Kinson*. BLSP. 1980.
McQueen, I. *Bournemouth St Peter's*. Dorset Publishing Co. 1971.
Mate, C. H. & C. Riddle. *Bournemouth: 1810-1910*. 1910.
Miller, G. *The Bournemouth Symphony Orchestra*. Dorset Publishing Co. 1970.
Morris, C. *History of Hants & Dorset Motor Services Ltd*. David & Charles. 1973.
Oakley, E. R. *The smugglers of Christchurch, Bourne Heath and the New Forest*. 1944, repr. 1945.
Official guide to Bournemouth. Bournemouth Corporation. Editions from 1905.
Parsons, J. F. *J. E. Beale Ltd and the growth of Bournemouth, 1881-1914*. 3 vols. BLSP. 1980-82.
Pevsner, N. & D. Lloyd. *Hampshire and the Isle of Wight*. Penguin Books. 1967.
Popham, Mrs C. *Rambling records of Stourfield*. c1930.
Popplewell, L. *Bournemouth railway history . . .* Dorset Publishing Co. 1973.
Popplewell, L. *Wick*. BLSP. 1979.
Ransom, W. P. *The story of Bournemouth Corporation Transport*. 2 vols. BLSP. 1982.
Russell-Cotes, Sir Merton. *Home and abroad*. 2 vols. 1921.
Sydenham, J. *The visitor's guide to Bournemouth and its neighbourhood*. 1st edition. 1840.
Tilden, P. *True remembrances: the memoirs of an architect*. Country Life. 1954.
Young, D. S. *The story of Bournemouth*. R. Hale. 1957.
Young, J. A. *Southbourne-on-Sea*. BLSP. 1978.
Young, J. A. *Victorian Boscombe*. BLSP. 1983.
Young, J. A. *The village of Pokesdown*. BLSP. 1979.
Young, J. A. *Winton and Moordown, 1894 to 1901*. BLSP. 1981.

(BLSP = Bournemouth Local Studies Publications.)

Directories
Hunt's Hampshire, 1851.
Kelly's Bournemouth, from 1899.
Mate's Bournemouth, from 1887.
Pigot's Hampshire, 1842.
Post Office Hampshire, 1859.
Stevens' Bournemouth, 1894-95.
White's Hampshire, 1859.

Newspapers
Bournemouth Daily Echo (now *Evening Echo*).
Bournemouth Graphic.
Bournemouth Guardian.
Bournemouth Observer.
Dorset County Chronicle.

This book uses much other source material in the Lansdowne Reference Library, Bournemouth.

Index

Subscribers

Presentation Copies

1 Bournemouth Borough Council
2 Dorset County Council
3 Lansdowne Library
4 Dorset County Library
5 Cllr Frank Beale
6 Cllr Michael Filer

7 David & Rita Popham
8 Clive & Carolyn Birch
9 Mrs J. Francis
10 David Grant
11 Mrs J. Dunster
12 Mrs S. Church
13 Mrs K. Bowyer,
14 Queen Elizabeth's School
15 H.S. Geneen
16 Mrs Dorothy Fox
17 Queensmount School
18 F.P. French
19 Miss B.A. Tavenor
20 Susan C. Topping
21 W.J.S. & C.L.E. Date
22 John & Pamela Evans
23 Wally Driffield
24 Miss J.M.B. Taylor
25 N. Heissig
26 Mrs Janet G. French
27 Mr & Mrs J.G. Hazell
28 G.H. Taylor
29 A.J. Hazell
30 Mrs P.M. Pike
31 Ian A. Taylor
32 Mr & Mrs Trim
33 Dr Frank R. Wadleigh
34 Mr P.A. & Mrs T.C. Barringer
35 J. Yates
36 G. Halstead
37 G.E. Armitage
38 Mr & Mrs J. Dicken
39 D.A. Eels
40 Charmaine Gordon
41 Mrs B.E.J. Day
42 Mr & Mrs R.G. Atkins
43 A.R. Philpott
44 Mrs S.E. Scott
46 R.D. Haskell
46 Mrs Jean Sutton
47 Eilen F. Brady
48 Mr & Mrs D. White
49 R.L. Eldridge
50 Mr & Mrs S.W. Warwick-Haller
51 Anne Salenieks
52 Mrs R. Olsen
53 R.A. Lambert
54 P.B. Bell
55 Robert John Foote
56 A. Connell
57 Miss G. Hayball
58 Nev Lewis
59 J.V. Boys MA
60 Mrs P. Weal
61 Peter Lord
62 F.V. Maring
63 Mrs Gwenda D. Dear
64 G.L. Pearce
65 W.L. Wright
66 I.P. Creese
67 Miss Janette Marsh
68 A.L. Young
69 R. Chorley
70 Brian Robinson
71 Mrs June P. Humphries
72 P.F. Thorne
73 Miss A.D. Welsher
74 P.G. Hayward
75 Paul Giddings
76 Miss W.M. Woolven
77 A.S. Dunstall
78 L.M. Francis
79 Elizabeth Edwards
80 Margaret Brown
81 Mrs A.P. Hockey
82 A. Maidment
83 Mrs P. Adams
84 Mrs Jean M. Day
85 H. Wheeler
86 Mr & Mrs L.R. Tarrant
87 Rev & Mrs E.A. Cowan
88 Mrs M.H. Stagg
89 Nigel Wickson
90 Jean Bartlett
91 R.A.H. White
92 L. Wilkins
93 Mrs J. Brookbank
94 F.W.G. Clayton
95 Miss J.K. Peart
96 Mr & Mrs J. Phillips
97 Mrs J.M. Cousins
98 Mr & Mrs K.V. Ward
99 Miss S. Gadd
100 Miss Rose Bentham
101 Roger F. Blake
102 Mrs M. Wetenhall
103 Paul Ekless
104 Jonathan M. Poulton
105 Mrs M.A. Chave
106 Mr & Mrs John Metherell
107 Miss R.M. Toconis
108 Paul Henry Miles
109 J.W. Morrell
110 Jenny Carpenter
111 D.C. Adams
112 Jeanne Etches
113 M.R. Briant
114 Patricia Butler
115 Ted & Daphne Gauntlett
116 Mr & Mrs Jukes
117 J.V.L. & E.M. Barker
118 Mrs E. Laurent
119 Mrs D.L. Andrews
120 Miss P. Williams
121 Mrs J.T. Mee
122 Bournemouth & Poole College of Art & Design
123 A.A. Young
124 Terrence F. Tuck
125 Miss L.A. Warwick
126 M.A. Edgington
127 John L. Matthews
128 L.R. Corner
129 Leigh Hatts
130 Mrs P. Perkin
131 Peter M. Mogridge
132 V.D. Ponton
133 Miss B.M. Ponton
134 Donald F. Sheppard
135 K.N. Cope
136 Stourfield Junior School
137 Mrs M.J. Browning
138 J.E. Pearce
139 Mrs Mary Knott
140 V.A. Shelton
141 Miss Doris Marshall
142 Miss K. Pawson
143 K.R. Barrett
144 S E Dorset Teachers' Centre
145 Helen Tilling
146 J.A. Young
147 F.L. Luckman
148 J.F. & N. Parsons
149 F.A. Williams & G.G. Williams
150 B.C. Langdown
151 Miss M.E. Roberts
152 Mrs P. Fairclough
153 Mrs V. Kingston
154 Miss C.J. Lewis
155 J.T. Robson
156 Mrs C. Mason
157 D.E. Lowe
158 Mrs H.A. Simmonds
159 Mrs K. Wilson
160 D.M. McIntyre
161 Miss R. Wright
162 Mrs Angela Brennan
163 Mrs B.I. Cowdrey
164 Mrs J. Sammonds
165 Mrs M.L. Thorne
166 C.N. Mentz
167 J.F.C. Fox
168 Herbert J. Ogden
169 N.G. Buchanan
170 Robert Charles Kelly
171 Mrs Valerie Clasby
172 Alan Dufall
173 Mr & Mrs J.F. James
174 Bournemouth Borough Planning Officer
175 Miss M. Jones
176 Miss N.L. Edwards
177 Mrs J. Kane
178 Mark B. Brown
179 Miss D.M. Gowlland
180 John P. Everitt
181 Mr & Mrs E.M. Baker
182 Mrs H.J. Howarth
183 David J. Morris
184 David King
185 Dr R. Hurst
186 Miss J. Knight
187 Miss Mary Nelson
188 Mrs Noreen Oliver
189 Mrs B. Potter
190 Miss F. Atkins
191 Mrs M.A. Cross
192 Lawrence Popplewell
193 Lesley Adams
194 T.W. Hall
195 Dr P.J.H. Barron
196 Mr & Mrs R.H. Addis
197 K. Silberman
198 Gordon Anstee
199 Mrs I. Peters
200 Zoe Mather
201 Mr & Mrs Samuel Dean
202 F.M. Kingsbury
203 Bob & Jean Nichols
204
205 Miss P.E. George
206 Roger Still
207 R.H. Hawkins
208 Gp Capt & Mrs C.E. Gould
209 Mr & Mrs M.J. Hill
210 Anne Sugden
211 A.J. Green
212 Mrs G. Morant
213 Mr & Mrs K.W.J. Lacey
214 Mrs R.B. Ridge
215 Lorna Rowlands
216 Jessie Cooper
217 Mrs J. Toalster
218 Miss Susan Cox

219 Miss R.M. Crossland
220 Miss Jeannette Simpson
221 Miss L.M. Rowe
222 Mr & Mrs K. Spencer
223 Mr & Mrs R. Watling
224 Mr & Mrs P. Hillier
225 Mr & Mrs J. Bean
226 C. Davey
227 C. Brockbank
228 Mr & Mrs G.W. Chamberlain
229 Mr & Mrs H. Notley
230 Mrs G. Edsall
231 J.B. Hawthorne
232 Sue Beaumont-Smith
233
234 David Comely
235 Iris A. Morris
236 J. Harris
237 Andrew D. Hawkes
238 D.R. Clark
239 Lord Eden of Winton
240 B. Black
241 Miss Barbara Eastwood
242 Mrs L.A. Watts
243 James F. Sullivan
244 Mrs Jean Roakes
245 Mr & Mrs D.G. Hilliam
246 Mr & Mrs Michael King
247 Mrs Patricia M. Voisey
248 Mrs A.M. Parr
249 W. Green
250 J.E. Brixey
251 Mrs M.K. Richards
252 David Halfpenny
253 Paul H. Miles
254 Dr Peter J. Barron
255 Mrs June Hughes
256 Sqn Ldr P.F. Christopher MBE DFC
257 Willoughby & Sons
258 P.F. Betteridge
259 John A. Hilton-King
260 Brian William Hall
261 David Trenchard
262 J.A.E. MacGregor
263 Gordon Anstee
264 Mrs Kitty Bristow
265 Frank Beale
266
267 Cllr A.G. Fudge
268 John Dixon
269 R.W.G. & M. Brown
270 A.W. Pinchbeck
271 Paul Shee
272 Dorset Natural History and Archaeological Society
273 Mrs T. Cook
274 P.F. Kellaway
275 Fox & Sons
276 Mary Michael
277 Allen Barnes
278 Priscilla Mary Gane
279 J.C. Mitton
280 G.W.J. Slade
281 Gp Capt W.J. Knowles RAF
282 Bernice C. Matthews
283 Mrs J.H. Barrett
284 Mrs E.R. Manwaring-White
285 F. Keetley
286 Brenda B. Didham
287 M.G. Key
288 Felicity A. Draper
289 W.H. Leach
290 W.J. Dyer
291 G.E. Hooper
292 W.J. Croom
293 F. Wiseman
294 Mr & Mrs K.J. Riley
295 E.V. Lawrence
296 George H. Chidwick
297 H.R.W. Harling
298 A.C. Farrell
299 Dorset Institute of Higher Education
300 R.A. Burden
301 Eda M. Farrell
302 M.N. Parsons
303 H.W. Perry
304 Mrs A. Gowman
305 Mrs Charles Gibson
306 Mrs Susan A. Simons
307 S. Draper
308 Paul Sillence
309 C. Adcock
310 Mary Broad Library, Talbot Heath School
311 G.M. Weston
312
313 E. Neville Jones
314 A. Zaccari
315 Donald Walter Hunt
316 D.F. Steele
317 Charles Henry Goddard
318 Mrs Sheila C. Coleman
319 Russell W. Harris
320 Christopher Williams
321 A., B., & A. Sklan
322 Derek Thompson
323 H.F.H. Burn
324 J.M. West
325 Mrs B.M. Reeve
326 Ralph Gordon Chambers
327
328 K.E.A. Barnett
329 Kenneth J. Mantock
330 Mrs Christine Kenny
331 R.J. & H. Singleton
332 Mrs Chisman
333 Mrs R. Bailey
334 Geoffrey Seddon
335 Cllr Richard Lee
336 M.A. Newman
337 R.E. Honess
338 Clive Lewis
339 P.K. Snooks
340 A.J. Hallock
341 Bournemouth School Library
342 F.C. Loxton
343 Colin Cope MA
344 Jill Kell
345 Derek C. Mills
346 R.C. Uren
347 M.A. Clarke
348 Anne Clarke
349 Annys Meadows
350 Bournemouth &
352 Poole College of Further Education
353 J. Read & S. Pennington
354 A.B. Ponchaud
355 Mrs V. Gerrard
356 E.J. Hayter
357 G.M.V. Cook
358
360 A.M. Twibill-Croft
361 E.J. Varney
362 Mrs D. Barry
363 The Librarian —
364 Canford School
365 Richard & Topsey Matanle
366 H. Cracknell
367 T.J. Franks
368 Patricia Moore
369 D. Fullock
370 Doug Blakman
371 Helen Solomon
372 Robert & Dorika Moore
373 Albert L. Fry
374 Mrs P.J. West
375 Lancaster Court Hotel, Bournemouth
376 Mrs Helen Pepper
377 Mrs J.I. Rawlins
378 Cllr P. & Mrs E. Real
379– Dorset County
433 Library
434 Mrs A.L. Whyborn
435 Mrs M.J. Tebboth
436 Mrs D.R. Litchfield
437 S.J. Gage
438 William J. Plumpton
439 P.H.M. Cooper
440 W.R. Green
441
442 D. Dobson
443 R.A. MacDuff
444 J.M. Flammery
445 Mrs Gurden
446 Peter Derek Couch
447 R.L. Jones
448 Miss M. Gard
449 John Gilbert
450 Ruth Taylor
451 Mrs Joyce Luminati
452 Mrs I.D. Evans
453 John Wilson
454 Jack & Norah Parsons
455 Mr & Mrs R. Brown
456 Peter McLean
457 Mrs J. Butler
458 J.D.R. Hankinson
459 Michael D. Read
460 Mrs P. Smith
461 B.E.N. Parker
462 Cyril Speller
463 Mr & Mrs W.A. Cotton
464 Sheila Savage
465 Eileen R. Calvey
466 K.G. Jewell
467 Clive Daniels
468 Ken & Fay Nicklen
469 Mrs Pamela Reeks
470 Jillian Sanford
471 Mrs A. Capon
472 Miss J. Goodwin
473 Miss J.M. Legg
474 Richard Pride
475 L.J. Clements
476 W.J. Whitelock
477 Leslie R. Coombs
478 G.C. Payne
479 Mary Plant
480 L.C. Shrimpton
481 C.J. York
482 Miss J. Warren
483 A.G.A. Mascarenhas
484 T.R. Hodges
485 Rissa Needham
486 Mrs E.A. Taverner
487 Mrs P. Harvey
488 Mrs M. Wheatley
489 Gray & Brooks
490
491 P. J. Jolliffe
492 Nicolas Ingleson

Remaining names unlisted.

[illegible]
Dorking
[illegible] 2008